INTERNATIONAL BUSINESS

Avison Wormald is a Visiting Fellow at the Centre for Contemporary European Studies, University of Sussex, a fellow of the British Institute of Management, and a member of their International Management Advisory Council. He obtained his BA with first class honours at King's College, London, and after a few more years of study, turned to business. In time he became a Managing Director of Fisons Ltd, and then Chairman of Grace Bros Ltd. In 1964 an undiagnosed heart condition forced him to give up full-time work for some years, and he became a self-employed consultant specializing in international business. His appointments in this capacity have included consultant to the Industrial Reorganization Corporation and adviser to the Council of Europe in Strasbourg. He has been for some years chairman of W. D. Scott and Co, the international management consultants. He has published many articles in management periodicals and contributed to *The State as Entrepre* ____ ___ ___ __ Stuart Holland.

GW00367463

Management Series

INTERNATIONAL BUSINESS

AVISON WORMALD

A PAN ORIGINAL

PAN BOOKS LTD : LONDON

First published 1973 by Pan Books Ltd,
33 Tothill Street, London SW1

ISBN 0 330 23569 9

Printed in Great Britain by
Richard Clay (The Chaucer Press), Ltd, Bungay, Suffolk

To John Marsh,
Director General,
British Institute of Management

Contents

Acknowledgements

In writing this book I have drawn principally on my own experience, but in one period of my life particularly, during my service with W. R. Grace & Co of New York, the atmosphere was so intellectually stimulating that some basic concepts of this book became much clearer to me than they had been previously.

I am indebted to the Chairman of the Board of that Company, Mr J. Peter Grace, Jr, for reading and approving those parts of the book which refer to his organization. Working there I saw the spirit of adventure which is perhaps the mainspring of international business, but also the shrewd eye watching the 'downside risk' without which the fun doesn't last long.

I am also much indebted to Dr Max Gloor of Nestlé Alimentana for the material which I found in his essay 'Policies and Practices at Nestlé Alimentana S.A.' and for reading the relevant parts of the manuscript.

It is a particular pleasure to thank Mr Roy Wright, Deputy Chairman and Deputy Chief Executive of RTZ, not only for permission to quote extensively from his *Policies and Practices of the Rio Tinto Zinc Corporation Ltd* but for reading the whole book in manuscript. His agreement with the main lines of my argument was a source of pride and encouragement to me.

I should also like to thank Professor Tibor Barna, Professor of Economics at Sussex University, and Mr Enrico Bignami, formerly managing director of Nestlé Alimentana, for their interest in the book.

Of course, most of a book like this one comes from the working of the unconscious mind in almost a lifetime of reading. The greatest part of that reading has been of the works of American scholars and, like many other managers, I owe a debt to the American Management Association of which I have been a member for many years, and also to the National Industrial Conference Board.

European scholars, notably Professor Dunning and Messrs Brooke and Remmers, have been active in this field, and the *Strategy of Multinational Enterprise* of the latter appeared when I was about halfway through the present book. I found it a great advance on previous works in this subject area and have drawn quite heavily on it.

To Dr Roy Pryce, Director of the Centre for Contemporary European Studies, University of Sussex, I owe my meeting with the advisory editors, Messrs Pocock and Taylor, and to them I owe the book itself, since their tactful patience kept me at work on it in the midst of many pressing preoccupations. Both of them read the whole of the manuscript and sent me valuable comments and advice.

The advisory editors complimented my secretary, Mrs Linda López Fonseca, on the appearance of the typescript, but they did not know of the editing, correction and comment which she also contributed.

Finally, I must not forget the assistance I received from the Library of the British Institute of Management and their excellently edited reading lists.

AVISON WORMALD

Introduction

Homo sum; humani nil a me alienum puto.
TERENCE

Business is an important socio-economic activity. As such it is concerned with a very wide spectrum of human life. It is a subject for the economist, the sociologist, the psychologist and many other branches of science. It is concerned with sex and religion, the bottom of the sea and outer space.

It is not surprising therefore that it can be described from many different standpoints, and books are written about it which are incomprehensible to all but a small number of specialists. The anatomist's view of a man is very unlike that of the psychoanalyst, but they are both talking about the same creature; they are merely looking at him with different pre-occupations in their own minds and seeing different things because their own backgrounds are different.

So it is with business, and with international business – the subject of this book. Most of the writers on the subject have been concerned with the environment of international business, because this is obviously different from that of the purely domestic activity. The best of these books are of interest to businessmen themselves, and they help them to see a pattern in their own fragmented experience. Then there is a whole class of indispensable books on such subjects as foreign exchange and other aspects of international finance.

The subject of international business, at least until very recently, was therefore made up of specialized knowledge or of discussions about the environment. Indeed, one distinguished American professor not long ago said it was in danger of becoming a minor branch of social anthropology. It is or was thus in the same state more or less as the study of business in general say twenty years ago. There was acknowledged to be accountancy and salesmanship, organization and research, but was there really such a thing as management, an element common to all these activities? There were brilliant efforts to distil some of the essence in such once-for-all works as *The Practice of Management* by Peter Drucker,* but really, until decision theory arrived via cybernetics, together with information techniques and some behavioural science work, there was not any such subject as management. There was some inspired personal guidance, but not much in the way of a structured discipline which could be steadily improved by the contributions of many hands and which concerned every aspect of the business. However, we now look, twenty years later, on a chief engineer or a chief accountant both as a highly skilled professional specialist and as a manager; there is an accepted corpus of knowledge concerning both roles and the argument now concerns not *whether* there is such a subject as management but *what* it is, and, still more, how much is essentially relevant to the everyday job.

This book is an attempt to take the newer subject of international management some way along the same road, that is, primarily to deal with some of the additional factors involved in the decision-making process, whether the decisions are about accountancy, investment, marketing or people. It does not deal in any depth with specialized matters, although I am hoping to do so in a further volume, but it looks at the process of executive decision-making in the international context, and stripped of its specifically specialized content. The concepts I discuss apply, I think, to any situation, with of course a different pattern of emphasis in each case. I am not concerned with the accounting or marketing methods of, say, the international oil industry, but I am interested to see that the balance of risk factors is very different, for example, from that of a fertilizer business, and indeed to note, with some surprise, that the oil business appears to be a relatively low-risk business, although

* Pan Books.

with a major element of rather specific kinds of uncertainty. If this is true (perhaps it is not), it is an important factor in the decision-making process at many different levels of the business. Even if it is not true, to determine which needs more specific knowledge of the business than I possess, I have at least isolated a problem and provided a tool with which to analyse it.

Although there is some inevitable overlapping with the problems of purely domestic business I have tried to concentrate on those features of international business management which are, in degree if not always in kind, rather specific to it. I have assumed, in other words, a broad acquaintance with the subject of business management in the domestic context, and have frequently taken concepts common to both domestic and international business and discussed only the international aspect.

This analysis is largely concerned with risk, communication and decision complexity, and it might be contended that these exist in every business situation and are not specific distinguishing features of international business. This is an objection which has caused me a good deal of concern, but on the other hand almost every work I have read *implicitly* accepts that these are features of international business which *in degree* render it different from business conducted in only one country. Professor Vernon refers to risk many times in his *Manager in the International Economy*, and this is a typical extract:

On the other hand, the decision-maker cannot confine his analysis to those elements of the problem that are amenable to a consistent and rational approach. He must take his problems as he finds them. And the problems that are identified with international business are shrouded, to more than the usual degree, with the uncertainty and risk that are endemic to most business decisions. Neither the structured disciplines nor the pragmatic professionals have very much to say to the student on this score. The disciplines generally tend to build their logical structures on propositions in which neither uncertainty nor risk is involved. And the pragmatic professional, operating out of a clinical experience that usually involves considerable exposure to uncertainty and risk, often has some difficulty in articulating just what his operating rules may be.*

A recent work, *International Financial Management*,† has three excellent chapters on 'environmental adversities', while Brooke and Remmers‡ discuss communication at length, and both risk and decision complexity are quite pervasive themes in their work.

The reader will quickly see that there are quite a few quotations in the book, but most of them are not from academic authorities. This is for the reason already mentioned, namely that not much has been written on this subject, but also that I am a practising businessman and I have therefore preferred to quote other businessmen or business publications. I am afraid I have worked some of them rather hard, partly because when they are good they are very good, but also for the reason that the same faces are so often seen on television – there are not many of them. I am grateful to Mr Roy Wright of Rio Tinto Zinc, to Dr Max Gloor of Nestlé and to Mr Clapham of ICI, and others, for their frequent appearances in the following discussion, although I am afraid they would (or will) complain that I have acted like the worst kind of television chairman, cutting them off just when they were going to say what they really meant.

A businessman has a rather characteristic attitude, after all, and while I have tried very hard to distil some general principles out of my experience, this is, I hope recognizably, the work of a businessman. I have spent more than twenty-five years on and off in the practice of international business. Most

* Raymond Vernon, *Manager in the International Economy* (Prentice Hall).
† David B. Zenoff and Jack Zwick, *International Financial Management* (Prentice Hall).
‡ Michael Z. Brooke and H. Lee Remmers, *The Strategy of Multinational Enterprise* (Longman).

capital cities in the world are pretty familiar to me and I have spent a lot of time just sitting in the home office, thinking and planning around the sort of question discussed in this book. I have therefore, as I say, insistently asked myself whether I have presented a valid analysis of the factors influencing the decision-making process. When I was setting up Tata-Fison in India, was I then concerned with these issues of communication, complexity and risk? When I was exploring the feasibility of a fertilizer plant in Brazil, were these the considerations in the forefront of my mind, however overlaid with local colour and idiosyncrasies? Were they, at least implicitly, present in those long and typically thorough executive conferences when I was working for W. R. Grace? I think they were, and if you assume all or most of the normal preoccupations of every businessman in addition to these specifically international elements, I think the general impression is true and reasonably well balanced.

Again, an important test which any valid theory of the subject must pass is whether it looks right, so to speak, from both ends of the telescope. Do these concepts only apply if our standpoint is the developed countries – the United States or the United Kingdom, for example – or is an Ethiopian or a Pakistani subject to the same pressures, dangers and opportunities? The description is very much coloured by my own personal experience, but on the whole the basic concepts seem to stand up quite well to this test. A businessman in Karachi engaging (as many do) in international operations would have no difficulty in acknowledging that communication, complexity and risk were matters that put his international business in a different category from purely local affairs.

In short, I think that these ideas represent part at least of a valid structure for the study of international business. Not indeed the whole structure, complete in all its details, but at least more than the architect's rough sketches, if less than his finished working drawings.

I am conscious indeed that this book presents rather a ragged appearance. I have tried to break new ground over a wide area, and to cultivate it all down to a fine level tilth would take more time and mental energy than I have at my disposal. I hope, however, that the basic concepts are right and that they are the ones that distinguish international from national business, at least more than others which could be identified, and always with the *caveat* that I am concerned with business management, not with economics, sociology, politics, international law or any of the other concerns which might legitimately be the subject of a book with the same title as mine. In the first chapter I have analysed in some detail the reasons why the theory of international business is not the same as that of international trade, and why the objectives of governments, while broadly consistent with those of business at the present time, are not invariably closely linked with them.

Nowadays the number of hands working at the common task is so large that every writer has to ask himself what compromise he must make with his ambitions in order that he should produce something even of transient interest and value. The material he has to deal with is constantly increasing, the perspectives change, and if he is not to be in a situation of constant revision he must be content with less than the whole truth and with less even than a really workmanlike job.

AVISON WORMALD

CHAPTER ONE

The Mainsprings of International Business

Why should international business be considered such an important activity? Perhaps for a small country like the UK the answer may be, in part at least, rather obvious: it needs raw materials, foodstuffs, tropical produce and even much specialized equipment. But does it *need* Fiat cars, Italian woollens and Japanese cameras; and does the United States need, in any meaningful sense, Volkswagen cars, Scotch whisky, French cigarettes? How is it that these questions are matters of high government policy, that ministerial or presidential pronouncements are made about them? And, assuming that they are needed, if only in the sense that someone would marginally prefer a Fiat car to a local British one or a Volkswagen to a 'compact', how is it that the individual businessman thinks it worth while to mount in meticulous detail enormously expensive operations in foreign countries, risking in some cases the stability or even the very existence of his company?

There are obviously two rather fundamental questions involved in this, one concerning the rationale of international trade, the other the motivation of the firm and the individual businessman. In this first chapter we shall look at some of the reasons underlying this complex activity.

The theory of comparative advantage
For the economist, the rationale of international business lies in the theory of comparative advantage, the same theory which in effect lies at the heart of all economic specialization. Countries, like individuals, are well advised, it seems, to concentrate on those things they do best, and, as far as they can, buy other things from someone else who will accept their products in payment.

Again and again we have seen how specialization increases productivity and standards of living. Now we must show exactly how this works out in the field of international or interregional trade, going behind the facade of international finance.

Why did the United States specialize a century ago in the production of agricultural goods and exchange these for the manufacturing output of Europe? Why is she today able to export highly complex mass-produced goods to the far corners of the globe? Why is the agriculture of Australia so different from that of Austria or Belgium? How great would be the costs of complete self-sufficiency to a modern country? How do all countries benefit from trade?

The key to the correct answers to such questions, and many more, is provided by the theory of comparative advantage or comparative cost. Developed more than a century ago by David Ricardo, John Stuart Mill, and other English followers of Adam Smith, the theory of comparative advantage is a closely reasoned doctrine which, when properly stated, is unassailable.*

Obviously there can only be a direct personal advantage if the buyer and seller are the same person, but in the Western world (not so much in Eastern Europe) buyers and sellers are different bodies and so these forces work through the market place and competition. One country exports motor cycles and, because of some advantage it possesses, these are more attractive in the other country than the domestic article, the sales of which decline, perhaps to a point (as in the United States at present) where domestic production virtually ceases. The exporting country finds itself, however, in the same position as regards computers, and imports these since they are superior to its own product. In this way both countries are likely to be better off, although in both cases there may well be complaints from injured manufacturers who may see themselves as more the

* Paul A. Samuelson, *Economics* (McGraw-Hill), p 64.

victims than the beneficiaries of the workings of comparative advantage.

There is a good deal more to the theory than this, and indeed, as is not unusual in matters of economic theory, some dispute as to the validity of the argument at the margin. We are here not greatly concerned, however, as of course the individual firm does not normally derive any direct benefit from this specialization. Governments on the other hand are very much concerned, but this is a matter of international trade policy, not business management. Consumers also are concerned, since if obstacles are placed in the way of international trade they have to be content with the locally produced article, good, bad or indifferent.

The individual businessman

From our point of view – the micro-economic – the businessman concerned with international business does what he does not because of any belief in the theory of comparative advantage but because the fact of comparative advantage provides him with an opportunity to exploit, in pursuit of something which motivates him more strongly, that is to say, personal advantage. The object of this chapter is to display the many forms which this personal advantage (or company advantage, of course) may take, and of which he will be conscious, as he is not conscious of the macro-economic forces shaping his environment.

There would probably not be much trade, in industrial goods at least, if there were no comparative advantage, but we have to look to other motivations in the case of the individual business and, indeed, businessman. His motivation may be partly, at least, one of the simplest and most basic, to which I certainly have been subject. International business to many is an extremely exciting activity. One must not underrate the importance of this element, even in the modern industrial executive, little as he may seem to have in common with those hardy travellers who, hundreds or thousands of years ago, penetrated into unknown and dangerous regions.

We take advantage of our operations around the world, and the exciting projects we have in hand, to attract men of high calibre within the UK and the countries where we operate . . .*

If the title of this book were *The Romance of International Business*, there would be an interesting story to tell.

Perhaps most boards of directors are ill-informed and apprehensive about business in countries other than their own, and indeed, as we shall see, this is in itself one of the major sources of risk – the fact that the corporate judgement is not broadly based as regards international business. In most businesses, then, which are successful in the international field there will be found some individual whose enthusiasm and knowledge are in fact the primary source of the effort which is made. Of course, this is to some extent the case with every activity, since each man cannot be equally informed about everything. In real life, however, the areas where there is most resistance to new initiative and bold schemes are science and international business, and for similar reasons. It is not common in writing on management to stress the difficulties of creating any forward-looking policy; indeed, the implication of most of the literature is that things happen when the technique and methodology are put in place, but this is because the most important factor, man himself, is the most elusive and difficult to analyse: '*merveilleusement ondoyant et divers*', as Montaigne put it.

We should not therefore allow ourselves to forget that somewhere in the complex motivation of international business will be found a creative urge to build a complete new business entity, which is a difficult thing to do in the domestic operations of even a medium-sized corporation. Both the planning and management of, for example, a new foreign subsidiary give opportunity for quasi-independent action and the hope of clearly attributable results within a reasonable time-span. The

* Roy W. Wright, *The Policies and Practices of the Rio Tinto Zinc Corporation Ltd* (published privately).

satisfaction of this creative urge is an important thing in the conditions of today.

The post-war environment

The businessman is shaped by his environment, by the economic and social forces of his time, and we will therefore set out briefly some of the main factors in this environmental situation.

The war of 1939–45 was undoubtedly a great watershed in the development of international trade and business. Before this period there had been the great depression of the thirties and trade had suffered heavily. There had been, as one economist put it, an international game of 'beggar my neighbour', with each country restricting its imports as far and as fast as it could. Large sections of the international economy, especially the Soviet Union, Italy and Germany, were practising policies of autarchy for a complex of economic, political and military reasons. This period is so distinct from that of the post-war that it hardly repays study except as an example to show where lack of international cooperation and short-sighted policies can lead.

In the post-war period there has been a great expansion of international trade and business, as the following table shows, and the reasons for this are complex: business has been both the beneficiary of forces not related to its activities and, in all probability, to some extent the promoter of this expansion. We are primarily concerned with the second order of causes, but both sets are interacting and repay study.

WORLD EXPORTS (FOB)

$ Billions

1950	1955	1960	1965
61·5	93·3	127·5	186·4

Source: OECD* at Work. March 1969

This represents in money terms a threefold expansion in fifteen years. Even allowing for inflation, this is a very high rate of growth.

* Organization for Economic Cooperation and Development.

Parallel with this growth of international trade is the growth of international direct investment, that is, investment made by individuals or companies in assets over which they will have some degree of continuing control.

The post-war period saw a conscious attempt to prevent the process of international impoverishment of the thirties from recurring and, largely under the influence of John Maynard Keynes, policies were agreed and institutions set up which have on the whole served the world rather well. The chief of these were the General Agreement on Tariffs and Trade (GATT), the Bretton Woods monetary agreement, the Marshall Plan and the International Monetary Fund. A number of other institutions of secondary importance followed, but we are concerned with the forces at work more than with the instruments through which they became effective.

Of course, there was also a great need for trade. A large part of Europe and Russia was devastated, food was short and the United States was called upon to play the role of enlightened promoter of world recovery.

After the war there appeared two main economic blocs: the Soviet (including Communist China and Eastern Europe) and the Western, around the United States. The trade between the blocs was limited for about ten years, until the death of Stalin in 1953. The great schism between the Soviet Union and China did not greatly increase the contacts of the latter with the Western world, but a series of events both loosened the control of the Soviet Union on Eastern Europe and led to increased trade between the Soviet Union and the West.

Simultaneously, and with the full support of the United States and the new international trading and monetary institutions, new regional blocs began to form in the West, and to a lesser extent in Asia. The most advanced of these is the European Economic Community, with the Latin American Free Trade Area seeking to emulate it, with somewhat limited success.

At times this process appeared to be running out of steam, but as fast as one front-runner, such as Germany, got a little out of breath, another – Italy, France, Spain or Japan – appeared. Monetary troubles threatened the success of the process, but first the US dollar and the pound, then the US dollar alone, and then a variety of expedients such as the Eurodollar, have filled the gap. For a quarter of a century, 1946–71, the world experienced a period of almost continuous economic expansion unprecedented perhaps in the history of man.

Businessmen who, as we have seen, suffer from the process of comparative advantage as often as they benefit from it, nevertheless supported it in a very large measure, and even invented ingenious expedients such as the Eurodollar (not a governmental invention) to deal with some of the difficulties arising for example from defects in the international monetary system.

It was only to be expected however that the attitudes of governments on the one hand and businessmen on the other should at times be strongly ambivalent. Governments are under numerous pressures, internal and external, while businessmen can hardly be expected to support with enthusiasm measures which do not benefit them fairly directly. There have been and will be therefore ebbs and flows in the tide of freer trade.

It is beyond the scope of this book to discuss the forces underlying the actions of governments tending to support freer trade. Certainly, political sensitivity to the threat of Soviet Russia motivated the United States in that critical quarter-century of 1946–71 to seek to unify the Western world and to avoid a repetition of the disastrous inter-war slump. There has always been a strong feeling that the Western world was on trial and that the free enterprise or capitalist system might not survive a slump of the same character as that of the thirties.

There was therefore in all this a set of motivations of a socio-politico-military character, largely but not entirely arising out of a confrontation between the two major powers of the world. But there were in operation equally strong forces, newer in character, supporting the same trend towards freer world trade and more international exchange.

Some of these things are obvious: the growth of wealth with

its concomitant need for more sophisticated goods; increasing leisure providing time for foreign travel; the exponential growth of the means of communication, and so on.

There has also been a marked change in the balance of forces in the world, even apart from the rise of Soviet Russia and later of China. The industrial preponderance of the United States has declined relative to that of Europe, Russia and Japan as a result of slower growth rates in the decade 1960–70 and the outlook is for a continuing shift in this balance.

The importance of technology

One of the most powerful underlying forces tending towards more international exchange and more international business has been, and will no doubt continue to be, a consequence of the growing importance of technology in the world. Now it is commonly thought that science and invention have followed the same course of evolution as industry, that is to say that success is a function of investment and other resources. This is undoubtedly true to a large extent but is by no means universally true. Relatively small countries have indeed been able to establish very important positions in specific technologies which are of great importance to *all* countries. The concept of autarchy in any given country in the post-war world would mean technical backwardness for that country in some important and perhaps vital sphere. It is quite true that the world is largely dependent on the United States for computers but no one assumes that this will necessarily continue. The most important post-war advance in steel-making occurred in Austria; Switzerland leads in pharmaceuticals and pesticides; Japan in some branches of electrical technology, and so on. Every country, even the largest and most powerful, is dependent on others for the products of technology. This accounts for the extremely rapid development of world-wide businesses such as IBM, Xerox, Hoffman-La Roche, Michelin and others – Japanese, Dutch or whatever.

The most recent studies appear to point clearly to a strong

COMPARISON OF GROWTH RATES OF OUTPUT 1960–1970
Previous Report and Latest Estimates

Average annual rates

	Weight in 1963	1960–65		1965–70 Previous Projection	1965–68 actual	1965–70 estimated
		Original	Revised			
		MAJOR COUNTRIES				
Canada	3·5	5·5	5·5	4·8	4·8	4·6
United States	52·6	4·5	4·8	4·5	4·7	3·7
Japan	5·9	9·6	10·1	7·5	12·5	12·4
France	7·4	5·1	5·8	4·8	4·5	5·4
Germany	8·3	4·8	5·0	3·5	3·2	4·4
Italy	4·3	5·1	5·2	5·0	6·0	6·3
United Kingdom	7·5	3·3	3·4	4·1	2·3	2·4
Total above	89·5	4·9	5·2	4·6	5·0	4·5

AVERAGE ANNUAL PERCENTAGE
RATES OF GROWTH OF GDP

	Estimate 1960–70	Projection 1970–80
	MAJOR COUNTRIES	
Canada	4·9	5·4
United States	4·2	4·7
Japan	11·3	10·0
France	5·6	6·0
Germany	4·7	4·6
Italy	5·7	5·6
United Kingdom	2·7	3·2
Total above	4·8	5·4

Source: The Outlook for Economic Growth – OECD May 1970

trend towards the faster development of trade in high technology products than in conventional products, showing that the newest trends are indeed the strongest.

Business and government on the same course

It is sufficient for our purpose to note that in the fifties and sixties, and perhaps with more hesitation in the seventies, there have been strong forces, political, social and technical, combining to favour the growth of international trade, and the businessman has responded to these forces, adding other motivations of his own not concerned with politics, the comparative advantage of the economists or the somewhat random nature of technological progress which we have just noted. His motivations are concerned with his own personal position and that of his organization. These might be conceivably in opposition to the prevailing trends. International business may experience strong countervailing forces in business in general, as it certainly does in particular businesses at particular times. When demand, for example, runs very strongly in the domestic market, *some* businesses lose interest in the more remote and hazardous operations of the outer world. Sometimes this counter-current is strong enough to provoke governments to action by pressures of various kinds – deflationary policies, the removal of protective tariffs, and so on.

But these are in general only partial and temporary movements and business and businessmen have found their own particular motivation for following the prevailing wind. It is these which are more particularly the object of our interest.

Types of international business

Most of what we have to say in this short book applies to all kinds of international business. At the same time, it is as well to bear in mind that businesses are very different in character, each with its own problems of management. Economic and management theory tend to deal in generalities but it is often of more interest to look at the behaviour of particular industries. In international business this is certainly so and we can see quite important differences of motivation and development between:

    trading organizations;
    raw-material and extractive industries;
    service industries;
    manufacturing industries.

Trading organizations

The statistics for three of the largest international trading groups based in the UK tell their own story:

	Rank by Turnover	Turnover £000	Capital employed £000
Metal Traders Ltd	20	388,024	8,931
C. Czarnikow	46	245,000	6,911
Bunge & Co	76	153,000	14,619

	Net Profit before interest, etc £000	Rank	Employees
Metal Traders Ltd	407	470	103
C. Czarnikow	543	458	233
Bunge & Co	313	379	544

(from *The Times, 1,000 Leading Companies in Britain and Overseas 1970–71*)

These three companies rank 20th, 46th and 76th in British industrial companies for turnover and 470th, 458th and 379th for profits. Their staffs at 103, 233 and 544 persons put them below the 500th company in this list (United Newspapers) which for a turnover of £17,105,000 and profits of £3,203,000 had 5,592 employees.

This is quite a typical profile of a world-wide trading business: a few highly expert staff, small fixed capital, huge turnover on which a tiny margin is earned (0·1%, 0·2% and 0·8% respectively).

Such businesses have in general several distinctive characteristics as regards their operations. In the first place, they are trading, that is, buying and selling goods which they do not produce, hardly ever handle or indeed sell physically. They are concerned with commodities, that is a relatively small number of things, largely raw materials such as metals, cocoa, wheat, which are natural substances, used for further processing or manufacturing. They are bought and sold according to a standardized description and quality.

These considerations mean that large areas of management, especially organization, marketing, production, personnel, research and development are not concerned. Financial expertise, however, is very important and certain aspects of risk management which we will be discussing are fundamental in trading operations.

Not a few of the major world-wide industrial enterprises of today have their roots wholly or partly in commodity trading. Unilever certainly has, although it has largely lost, relatively recently, the rather distinctive style of a trading concern. Shell Transport and Trading preserves the trading connexion in its name, and important industrial concerns such as W. R. Grace still have a carry-over of trading attitudes which is quite significant in their make-up. They sometimes bring to the acquisition of businesses, for example, the same caution and consciousness of the 'downside risk' which is characteristic of trading concerns, and perhaps are still to some extent traders in businesses rather than industrialists. The polished business school graduate may have supplemented rather than replaced the shrewd trader.

The greatest obstacle to permanent establishment in a foreign country is unfamiliarity with the local environment. Trading businesses, however, acquire naturally, almost as it were by a process of osmosis, familiarity with other countries than their own and thus they frequently become established in them. Trading houses establish a foothold, this becomes consolidated by the purchase of local businesses, and in time there may be a fully fledged international organization such as the huge, largely privately owned, Vestey organization, with interests in every aspect of meat production, transportation and distribution.

Raw-material and extractive industries

Many of these businesses (we have instanced Shell) may have a strong trading element in their management make-up, but in so far as their mining or extractive interests are concerned they are at the other end of the scale with important fixed assets located mostly outside their country of origin.

	Turnover £000	Capital employed £000
Shell	2,352,250	1,909,593
Rio Tinto Zinc	338,046	574,830 *

In the one case a capital intensivity of nearly 1:1, in the other of nearly 2:1.

* Source: *The Times, 1,000 Leading Companies in Britain and Overseas 1970–71.*

These are businesses that operate outside their own country as it were from choice – not to increase markets, spread overheads or preserve an existing position against the threat of tariffs.

They tend to think in terms of very high risk because of the size of investment and the time span, to which must frequently be added a measure of political risk also. It is certainly not accidental that concepts such as discounted cash flow, emphasizing the time element in the return on investment, have been pioneered by mining finance enterprises. Indeed, an official of the Rand Mines in South Africa told me that these techniques were in use there in the 1920s, while Rio Tinto Zinc was certainly one of the earliest companies to use them extensively.

These are high-risk * businesses therefore, from whatever angle they are looked at – exploration, exploitation, investment, markets or politics. It is hardly surprising that some of the most colourful international figures, often with an obvious streak of

* Here 'uncertainty' is subsumed under 'risk'.

adventurer, have been prominent in this kind of activity. Whatever precautions are taken, with all the refinements of modern science, the motive must remain highly speculative.

There is much to be learned from the operations of the mining finance houses; we have already quoted Mr Roy Wright of Rio Tinto Zinc, one of the great mining finance houses of the world, and will do so frequently as our discussion proceeds.

Service industries, including international communications

Sea and air transport, postal and telecommunications services are in quite a special category, being essential to the maintenance of any international contact. As such they are, to a greater degree than almost any other international activity, governed by detailed and almost universal agreements.

The growth of service industries – advertising, banking, transport, tourism and so on – in the advanced industrialized countries has been accompanied by a rapid growth in international business. In the main this reflects the growth of international trade and investment and indeed of tourism itself, which is an important consumer of other services such as banking and transport.

Service industries, while obviously not by any means a homogeneous group, have certain things in common as regards their overseas operations. They operate outside their own country largely in order to supply a service to people or organizations of their own nationality. Every postal service exists to serve the people of its own country who wish to send letters abroad, and to receive them. The same applies to telecommunications.

The business of a tour operator is to convey its own nationals abroad and to supply their wants. Even advertising agencies and banks frequently establish overseas businesses in order to give service to their domestic clients. Once established in foreign countries they may acquire clients in those countries, and indeed frequently do, but this is not their primary motivation in setting up abroad. Indeed, since service businesses by definition provide service, they are apt to have certain disabilities in operating in foreign conditions where the requirements of customers may be different, corresponding to a different social, cultural or business set-up. They therefore frequently bring no major skill or knowledge sufficient to give them some local superiority, but on the contrary have to learn how to operate their businesses in very different conditions.

Manufacturing industries

The motivation of the company and the executive in the case of the three types of business we have considered, trading, extractive and service, is obviously not uniform. The mining engineer, in theory at least, seeks his preferred mineral wherever it may be found; the trader's contacts may be limited to telephone, cable and letter; the provider of services is serving his domestic customer, not an overseas customer, and this is basically so whether he is concerned with communications, holidays, or banking and insurance services.

The position of the manufacturer is more complex, and while of course some of the more basic motivations are common to all forms of overseas business, the manufacturer differs in one essential feature from the others whom we have described. It is only exceptionally that he is in the foreign market to serve a domestic customer – it can happen, for example, in the case of a manufacturer who sets up a plant abroad for which he needs parts or materials. His home supplier follows him to supply the same parts as he does in the home market. But this is exceptional, and the most important reasons for manufacturing industries being concerned with international business spring from the economy of the business itself. As we shall see later, frequently the stimulus comes from outside – an approach from an import agent abroad, new tariff restrictions, or a variety of other reasons – but the essential causes are the benefits to the economy of the business, of a most complex and varied kind. It is manufacturing business, therefore, which forms the principal study of this book.

When trade in manufactured goods became of some importance markets were extremely imperfect in the classical economic sense; that is to say that, because of poor communications, there was very little knowledge of other goods of the same kind which might be available. Travelling salesmen and trade fairs, which have always been a feature of international trade, helped in some degree to improve this situation.

In these circumstances export trade in manufactured goods was conducted largely because of high profits, the manufacturer or an intermediary selling to an eager buyer who had little knowledge of, or access to, alternative sources. Very high profits were also among the recognized rewards for personal hazards and the business risks involved in foreign trade. The life-span in India of the European might only have been four or five years a century ago, but he expected in that time to make a substantial fortune to take home. This situation exists to some extent at any time, but it now tends to be exceptional, and in many cases profits on export business are lower than on domestic business, a situation which we will look at later.

It is true that, as we have seen, there are in many cases powerful environmental pressures impelling the industrialist to export or trade abroad, but obviously if he is going to endure the special hazards of international business, which are indeed one of our main themes in this book, as well as a variety of other inhibiting factors, there must be important reasons of a fundamental kind.

Economies of scale

The economist, or at least the industrial economist, would point in the first place to the *economies of scale*. In general, if with some reservations, the businessman thinks that more sales produce lower costs, through lower prices for raw materials (purchased on a larger scale), longer runs on plants, a spreading of overhead costs, and so on. There is no doubt that this is, at one stage at least of the development of an international business, a very powerful motive. Because of this belief, and within certain limits, the businessman will accept in some cases prices which only make a contribution to his fixed costs: he will be prepared to forgo any profit at all. In the next chapter –

'Phases in the Development of an International Business' –
we will explore the limits of this approach, since obviously he
cannot be prepared in any circumstances to make sales at less
than full costs, let alone with no profit. Such a policy could lead,
and frequently does, to an overall loss for the company as a
whole.

In the case of exports this policy may be obvious enough: by
selling more of his products in foreign markets, assuming that
this is easier than in the home market, the manufacturer reduces
his overall costs, even if the foreign sales show him lower margins. In this way his profitable sales are made more profitable.
He takes his profit on the domestic market, using perhaps, at
the worst, the overseas market as a means of reducing his
costs.

But when he is manufacturing abroad, as he may be com-
pelled at some stage to do, how then does he obtain any economies of scale? This may in fact be a difficult question to decide,
especially if it costs more, as it often does, to do the foreign
business than the domestic. This is where an apparently in-
exorable law of modern business comes into play and provides
a powerful motivation which may not have influenced earlier
generations to the same extent.

Direct and indirect costs

It appears to be a principle of wide, if not perhaps universal,
application that the proportion of indirect or overhead costs to
direct costs is steadily increasing. Obviously these costs are to
some extent a function of the size of the business, and small
businesses generally point to 'lower overheads' as a convincing
reason why they are more efficient. It is true that in some proportions, difficult to define exactly, the mere cost of administra-
tion is an important element in production costs, and large
companies may be severely disadvantaged in this respect for
certain types of manufactures.

But it is nowadays not merely larger size which produces this
larger element of overhead costs; it is a change in the nature of
business itself. It is a pervasive change, and we will take only

the most obvious aspects of it, research and development, as exemplifying the general trend.

The chart opposite shows the rapid increase in research and development (R and D) expenditures in some OECD countries in the post-war period. This is obviously not all industrial research by any means; in the US and UK at least a substantial part is defence spending, but still the trends do broadly represent the increase in industrial spending.

Some industries spend 15 or 20 per cent of sales revenue on R and D, and these sums have become so large in absolute terms that only the State can support the expenditure. Few industries spend nothing and the average may be around 2–3 per cent for all industries.

The financial return from virtually any kind of technical advance is proportional to the volume of production to which it is applied. This is not quite an absolute law, but it is almost so. If, for example, a technical change in a process reduces costs by 5p a pound (weight), then the return is 5p for *every* pound manufactured. Clearly, therefore, apart from any other consideration, the larger a company's sales are the more revenue it derives from its technology.* There is frequently confusion about this simple issue and percentages are quoted as being appropriate to research expenditure in various kinds of industry - for example 1% of sales in the heavy chemical industry and 10% of sales in the pharmaceutical industry. Now clearly there is very little meaning in this kind of statement because the sum needed to make a particular technical improvement is not a relative sum but a definite sum of money, other things being equal. There are in fact two forces pulling in the same direction in all technically based industry: namely, the desire to exploit to the maximum every technical advance and the desire to increase sales in order to spread the burden of overhead costs, of which research is frequently one of the most important, and thus provide funds for still more R and D.

Frequently the threshold costs of establishing a position in

* See quotation following from Chairman of Unilever Ltd, Annual General Meeting, May 8th, 1972.

Gross national expenditure on research and development as a percentage of gross national product at market prices (source, OECD).

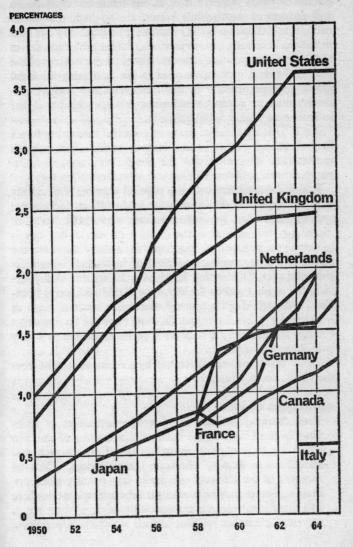

a research-based industry, that is, the minimum costs which will produce a worth-while result, are so high that international specialization is the result, with perhaps only one firm in the world making certain products. Patent protection serves to reinforce this position although it is often the weakest of the various forms of protection open to the innovating business. Conversely, particularly in small countries like Switzerland, involvement in advanced industries is only possible if the international market is the objective.

R and D is then one of the most powerful motivating forces in international business and it is not surprising that research studies tend to confirm that the fast-growing areas of international trade are those dealing with advanced technology.

R and D concerned with the physical sciences is obviously only one aspect of the 'knowledge business', and increasing specialization even in such relatively unscientific areas as marketing has resulted in the creation of very strong quasi-monopoly or oligopolistic positions. Frequently these are the result of a fairly complex mixture of ingredients – product characteristics, distribution know-how, advertising skills, service, and so on. Perhaps the arch-type of this situation is Coca-Cola, although there are many others less obvious, such as Volkswagen or Shell gasoline. In these cases the total product concept is sufficiently strong for it to be applicable to a very wide variety of markets.

These points are well illustrated by a recent statement from the Chairman of Unilever:

Advantages of scale

Your company benefits from certain advantages of scale. Only in the US or in the enlarged Community of the Ten could a purely national company spend on research and specialized services on the scale Unilever does. The total turnover of the Unilever companies in a country like Denmark or Greece may be smaller than the total spent elsewhere in Unilever on research and specialist services which are in one way or another relevant to their activities. Expenditure on detergent research of general application would eat up the profits even of a big company like Lever Brothers in the UK, if it had to pay for all of it alone; and even our biggest margarine companies might have hesitated before employing forty people over most of the 1950s on scientific research to blitz the problem of the flavour of margarine, as did Unilever; and which single food company could have contemplated expanding this effort by a further twenty people in the 1960s, to cover the whole wide field of food flavours? And what purely national company outside America could afford to spend £650,000 per year on the biological testing of the safety of its products and £600,000 on nutritional studies?

The economies of scale in research and specialized central services owe their importance to a very simple principle. Knowledge has no marginal cost. It costs no more to use it in the 70 countries in which we operate than in one. It is this principle which makes Unilever economically viable.*

In the majority of cases the natural pull will be towards less sophisticated markets than where the knowledge 'package' originates, and undoubtedly the search for 'softer', less competitive markets has prompted a good deal of exploration of international markets, from the US to Europe, from Europe to Africa, India and South America, and so on. The move towards 'harder' markets, such as from Europe to the US, particularly strong in the post-war years, has of course been due to other factors, primarily the opportunities of the largest and richest market for most goods in the world, but also frequently to the desire to become involved in a situation where there was so much to be learned, albeit with great difficulty and risk. Such a motivation was no doubt a powerful contributory factor in the move of Olivetti to the US through the purchase of Underwood.

Economies of scale, then, whether as a motivation towards export trade, through traditional manufacturing economies, or

* Unilever Ltd. Statement of Chairman of the Annual General Meeting, May 8th, 1972.

working through this new structural principle of sophisticated business, are one of the most powerful forces impelling a business to expand, wherever it may be.

Other motivations

Foreign trade tends to be a small proportion of total trade in very large countries such as the United States or Soviet Russia, at least as far as can be seen at present. It has to be remembered, however, that both countries are relatively 'new' countries compared with the older industrial countries. At the same time, if we are right in supposing that the somewhat random development of science and technology is in fact a valid principle, then it is likely that even the largest countries will have increasing requirements for imported products. Obviously, however, advanced industrial countries of small or medium size such as Sweden, Switzerland, Holland and England are likely to have a greater incentive to trade than the very large, richer countries. The search for larger, richer markets, therefore, in the case of industrialized countries, must be counted as a powerful motive, and as one independent of the economies of scale. Once a company develops expertise in selling or operating in foreign markets then it tends to be a self-generating process to some extent, those executives who have developed the expertise tending to look for new and challenging opportunities.

The role of agents

All writers on this subject stress the relatively fortuitous character of much early involvement in foreign operations and we will develop this theme in the following chapter. The proverb of the mousetrap* is indeed true to a large extent as regards foreign trade because of the existence of so many traders whose business is importing and distributing foreign products. They play a very important role in the development of foreign business and so we shall look at this process now in more detail. This will lead us to examine those more specific

* 'If a man made a better mousetrap, the world would beat a path to his door.'

motives which result in the establishment of manufacturing businesses in foreign countries, whereas up to now we have been considering rather generalized motivations concerning export sales as well as any other kind of overseas activity.

Agents are generally found to be more satisfactory in the early stages of the business since they frequently exploit actual or latent demand, making little contribution to promotion. Their shortcomings are apt to appear when the business develops. If the business is of any size, the manufacturer requires a sales forecast on which he can base his manufacturing programme. The agent is, however, frequently only used to the 'indent' system, whereby he places orders but looks no further ahead than the immediate requirements of customers on the one hand, and the logistics of delivery on the other, require him to do.

The result of this method of operating is generally dissatisfaction all round: for the customer because he may get poor delivery; for the agent because he loses sales, and for the manufacturer because he cannot plan ahead.

The commonest causes of dissatisfaction are the shortcomings of agents in regard to promotion and service. Frequently they are not set up to handle either of these matters satisfactorily and, in the absence of long-term commitments from the principal, do not wish to commit themselves, while manufacturers are generally reluctant to enter into long-term commitments without having control.

Halfway arrangements are not uncommon, whereby promotion is a joint responsibility, the manufacturer having his own representative in the offices of the agent to look after his interests, make sure the market is exploited to the best advantage, and advise on promotion. Frequently, however, such arrangements are resisted by the agent who, rightly, thinks the manufacturer will get to know too much and will eventually be in a position to dispense with his services.

The agency business tends, therefore, to be a shifting one, losing business to manufacturers' own local organizations once it reaches a size which justifies setting these up; conversely, an agent frequently sets up plants to manufacture products which he formerly handled for other firms. Some of the large Indian agents have shown a fairly consistent pattern of this kind and are now important local manufacturers in their own right, or associated with firms for which they formerly acted as agents.

The form of organization – representation, branch or subsidiary company – under which the move abroad takes place is relatively immaterial; the important fact is the increased commitment to the business in the market and the generally increased ability to handle it and extract the maximum from the particular market situation. There is now likely to be a much more positive pressure on the home organization than previously, as individuals acquire a personal interest in increasing the size and scope of the new organization. This, as everyone who has been concerned with international business will know, constitutes probably the most powerful motivation in the situation. Such positions, representing the company in developing foreign markets, tend to be filled by individuals more independent and aggressive than the average, and many companies trace their position in foreign markets to individuals whom they have sent to represent them in this way.

The move to the host country

A feature of the post-war situation has been the very large increase in 'direct investment', that is, investment made chiefly by industrial concerns setting up facilities abroad which they then own and operate. Previously, although to a declining extent, investment had not been linked to the ownership of facilities, and indeed had taken the form of bond issues in many cases.

Since the war the major investor has been the United States and the reasons for this investment have been investigated by the National Industrial Conference Board.* Tariff restrictions and transport costs were the most frequent. Other reasons were lower manufacturing costs abroad, involvement in growing

* *US Production Abroad and Balance of Payments* (National Industrial Conference Board, 1966).

markets and access to R and D information.

The imposition of tariffs, sometimes in isolation or sometimes allied to a government decision to see a particular industry established, is a powerful factor in impelling a manufacturer with an established sales position to set up a manufacturing operation. In many cases it has been the only factor, since the operation has been judged to be uneconomic even with tariff protection. The rayon industry in Australia is a well-known example, and motor-car assembly in a number of South American countries. In these cases, if the manufacturer sets up a facility he may do so only to conserve his market position against the day when the position may change, either by the growth of the market or the elimination of the tariff, permitting a return to importing.

If the venture is judged to be particularly unpromising, as it was in the case of rayon in Australia, then the commitment is frequently reduced by the introduction of local capital, or by an arrangement with local interests for manufacture under licence. With both these arrangements the future can be safeguarded to some extent by maintaining a degree of control which will enable the principal to improve his position if circumstances should justify it. He may, for example, introduce only loan capital, if local finance regulations allow it, or the licensing arrangements may only be for a term of years, provision being made for compensation in the event of termination, and so on. The English Ford Company had, for many years, a substantial participation of local equity shares, bought out by the parent company when the requirements of intercountry integration seemed likely to be incompatible with local shareholdings.

Obviously the threat of loss of a valuable market is a powerful incentive, in whatever form it may present itself, and it may well be that this has been the major factor in determining businesses to establish themselves in their foreign markets to manufacture, wholly or partially, products which they had previously imported. It is not, however, the only such motive; the cost of transportation, lower local costs of manufacture, and the need for different types of products are all important factors of a more positive kind. Until very recently at least the cost of transportation of liquid ammonia was such as to preclude its export to distant countries, and it was necessary to manufacture it locally if a place in the market was sought.

Lower costs of manufacture may well be found when either labour or material costs are substantially below those of the exporting country. The balance in some cases is fine, higher depreciation costs, for example, in the new market offsetting lower material or labour cost; in this case the manufacturer has to look to the future and decide which of his major costs are likely to move favourably and which unfavourably. If he is exporting to Italy he may be tempted by low Italian wage rates to set up local manufacture, but when he looks at the rate of increase of Italian wages compared with the trend in his own country he may decide that the advantage will not be permanent.

We have mentioned different types of products, and this is indeed a frequent reason for setting up local manufacture. If the company is in the consumer-products field for example, it may consider its principal asset to be marketing skill, applied to a wide range of products in its particular area. In that case it may lose little by manufacturing a rather different range of products in the foreign market, provided that its characteristic marketing skills are used. This line of argument (if we substitute design and production skills for marketing), would apply to the American automobile manufacturers in Europe. The Ford range in Europe in the sixties and seventies has consisted of cars designed especially for the European market. If the duty position had been different there would have been some question as to whether this range of cars should be made in America and imported into Europe. Such a decision would have meant that Ford would have cut itself off from that intimate involvement in the European market which has enabled it to compete very successfully with native European manufacturers.

In this type of situation the motivation for the move abroad

is obviously not simple and there is a long list of pros and cons
to weigh up. The defensive reaction towards the possible threat
to an established market is certainly a powerful factor, but the
necessity to become intimately involved in the local market is
also important in many cases. The foreign company may be
recognized as such in many cases, but the fact that it is established as a complete business, perhaps employing many local
people, means that it has a different image in their eyes from
that of an entirely foreign-owned and foreign-made product.
The involvement of the foreign company is, moreover, likely
to be much more continuous, and it will benefit from its
progressive integration into all phases of the national life. Any
business which affects the national life of the host country to an
appreciable extent has, therefore, to consider carefully whether
there are not important considerations, not of an immediate
economic character, which should influence it in the direction
of local establishment.

Positive pressure by foreign countries

The threat to established market position is obviously a kind of
negative pressure. The foreign company yields to pressure and
does what it regards as advantageous – the lesser of two evils.
But governments frequently use more positive inducements,
to attract foreign industry to their countries, or to specific
areas of them. There is no doubt that in European countries
generally the advantages offered as part of regional development policies have proved particularly attractive to foreign
firms, while some particularly under-developed areas have
benefited from the offer of tax holidays, loans at low rates and
similar inducements. On the whole, American companies
appear to have weighed up these advantages more carefully in
making up attractive investment packages. The establishment
of a large-scale ammonia industry in Trinidad depended, for
example, on a sophisticated package of local costs: low gas
price, tax holidays and technical progress in transport.

Financial motivations

No doubt the oldest and largest international companies have long been conscious of the possibilities latent in the lack of harmonization in tax laws between most countries. A state of affairs where most companies are aware of these possibilities is a comparatively recent phenomenon, and has found a powerful stimulus in the combined pincer movement on profits exerted in the post-war period by lower returns on capital, inflation and high taxation. The maximization of profits and minimization of taxes has become almost a condition of survival of many industries in these conditions. Enormous ingenuity has been exercised in causing profits to arise in low-tax areas, whatever the true source might be, and keeping them out of reach of the government in the domestic country. There is at least an impression that this policy tends to be pushed to its logical conclusion where the motive is strongest, ie, with very large family or personally owned businesses. A concentration of assets in one country would attract the attention of the authorities and, where taxation is highly progressive, would prevent the conservation of profits and, frequently, assets. Such circumstances explain the otherwise curious fact that Switzerland has long been a very important investor in Italy. The fact is that this is Italian money held in Switzerland and reinvested in Italy.

Italian funds in Switzerland – Swiss funds in Panama, which is the seat of one of the Nestlé holding companies. Switzerland is a low-tax area but is certainly not tax free, and there are, no doubt, other reasons why some at least of the funds of Switzerland's largest company should be held in a neutral zone. In recent years, at least, taxation, exchange and other financial controls have been factors in the internationalization of business.

Conclusion

If we look at the motivations influencing international business we see that, apparently at least, they have little to do with the economists' theory of comparative advantage. We see individuals and corporations actuated by a great variety of motives of self-interest, some of which seem directly opposed to the interests of their own country. Directly, at least, the theory of comparative advantage only comes into play within very large multi-national corporations which may be able to specialize in the production of components or their equivalents in the most economically favourable conditions.

The fact is that the intervention of money has divided the economic interest, the sellers of one type of goods in one country having no direct relationship with the sellers of other goods in another country. Prices to some extent bridge the gap, since a country very unfavourably placed for the production of one type of goods will find it better to buy these and to sell other goods which it is better fitted to produce, and the prices of which are therefore more competitive. But the individual seller, grower or manufacturer is not consciously concerned with this process in most cases. The theory of business is therefore a different theory from the theory of trade.

The motivations are obviously rather heterogeneous and of differing importance in the case of different companies. Some indeed have little choice about becoming international or multi-national; tourist businesses and airlines are in most cases not likely to be content with their home markets. Companies with a backward integration into raw materials, such as Unilever or the aluminium companies, are not likely merely to buy or mine; they will become sellers also. Many companies are naturally international, but many are not, and when they are not it is frequently for a complex of reasons, or under pressure, that they move abroad. The economic laws in this situation are mostly obscure and chance plays a larger role than planning in most cases.

Governments in general strive to encourage international trade, and indeed government interest in foreign trade has a long history. In the past there have been in most countries periods of isolationism and doubts about the advantage of trade, but they seem to have been passing phases.

The interest of businessmen in trade has undoubtedly had different origins, but where the trader himself benefited from the law of comparative advantage, being himself both a buyer and a seller, in a way that the modern corporation generally does not, his experience and interest ran parallel to that of his government. In the modern world, as we have seen, the businessman derives little or no apparent advantage from the workings of comparative advantage – indeed he may often feel that he is the victim rather than the beneficiary of his government's belief in freer trade. But he has developed a new and complex motivation, not replacing so much as strengthening his instinctive search for expansion and even adventure.

The attitude of governments to imports has perhaps been more generally ambivalent than towards exports. Some have been seen as highly desirable, others less so, but it has generally been recognized that some accommodation was necessary between the desire of the seller to sell what *he* wanted to sell, and that of the buyer to buy what *he* wanted to buy.

Since the motivation of governments and businessmen is not the same under the conditions of the present day, it is inevitable that there should be conflicts over a number of issues. Whether these are greater than they were is a question for the economic historian to consider; it may well be that they are.

Some of the conflicts arise obviously from the size and power of modern corporations, equalling in some cases that of national states, which are considered to be themselves of importance in world affairs. We shall see, moreover, that this conflict is not restricted to the receiver, as it were the 'host' country, but the existence of these 'states within a state' can create problems for the domestic governments themselves. The multi-national corporation can take some advantage from its ambivalent status as a national corporation in many countries, regulated to some extent by the laws of that particular country, but also enjoying a kind of extra-territoriality, where there is little or no law.

Again, the state places a higher value on its national security than do some businessmen, at least, and so there is a certain divergence of views in a number of countries about the export of strategic products and materials to countries which may be potential enemies, and even to some which are certainly friends.

The export of capital is another area where governments are not uniformly favourable; some, such as those of Eastern Europe, are definitely unfavourable while others, such as the United States, which have been extremely liberal, have lately had to restrain the ardour of their businessmen but have not been too successful in restraining their ingenuity.

On the whole, in describing the background to international business, we have been inclined to stress the concordance of aims of governments and businessmen which, when the main common aim – comparative advantage – appears to have virtually disappeared, is rather remarkable. It is important therefore to mention, as we have just done, that if there are parallel and convergent aims, there are also some that diverge.

Further reading
Raymond Vernon, *Manager in the International Economy* (Prentice Hall).
Charles P. Kindleberger, *International Economics* (Richard D. Irwin).

CHAPTER TWO

Phases in the Development of an International Business

Having looked in a general way at the forces, external and internal, which motivate international business, it may be instructive to trace the process at work in a kind of generalized 'model'. We have discussed the influence of many highly disparate elements which may be operative, but the way in which these may combine to produce a kind of living organism is perhaps better shown by this means.

It has been noted by a number of writers that in the early stages at least the basic decisions about a company's international activities are brought about by external forces; that is, there is no conscious policy at all. A company making some product purely for domestic consumption may receive an inquiry from an overseas buyer or is approached by an agency company to sell the product abroad. Very few companies in the world have obviously started operations with the definite objective of serving an international market, rather than a domestic market plus *some* export or overseas manufacturing. Obviously the large multi-national corporations now plan their operations on a world-wide basis, not based on any one home market. A number of Swiss and Swedish companies, and others in small countries, regard themselves as entirely multi-national, but this is perhaps not how they started.

It has been said that man climbs his own genealogical tree, that is, from birth to maturity he evolves through all the stages which have brought him from a relatively low level in the zoological world to his present position in the hierarchy of animals. Similarly, very many business organizations engaged in international business evolve through the different phases which have characterized the growth of international business as an activity. A useful methodological approach therefore is to consider this evolutionary process and the different policy questions and options which occur at each stage, as a preliminary to some more detailed inquiry into certain specific aspects.

Some of the decisions are obviously fairly arbitrary; in practice, the cases where some of them at least are discrete entities may be comparatively rare, but there are clearly stages in an evolutionary process where the changes do appear to be particularly significant and it is these which we have tried to isolate, while being conscious of the essential oneness of the process.

PHASE I – OPPORTUNISM

We have referred incidentally to what is in many cases the first phase (sometimes also the last) in the evolution of an international business.

A company, generally small, is manufacturing a product for a domestic demand; it may have no interest in developing alternative markets or may not see the possibilities; it may have considered the possibility but decided against it. An example might be a manufacturer of specialized surgical instruments. A range has been developed to suit the technique of a local specialist and by word of mouth a market has been developed. It might well be considered that there was no export market of interest in their range, because:

(a) the techniques of foreign surgeons are probably different;
(b) instruments are hand-made by skilled craftsmen and probably each main centre abroad has such an established instrument industry.

A foreign surgeon, however, has seen the instruments in a London hospital and tries to obtain them in his own country because they are:

(a) better than local instruments in design and workmanship;
(b) cheaper because of differential wage rates.

He tries to get them from a prominent local supplier, known to be a dealer in imported instruments, but fails to obtain them. The dealer's interest is, however, aroused and he writes to the English manufacturer, requests particulars and inquires about the possibility of becoming the local agent.

The English manufacturer is surprised, flattered and pleased to get this inquiry, and replies that he is willing to give an agency. From this point he becomes involved in a whole series of policy decisions, often with a growing sense of frustration and the feeling that it is more trouble than it is worth. Without going into all the minutiae of such transactions – import licences, even postal regulations – some important policy questions have to be faced.

Products
Will he sell the full range he sells in England? If he does, it may involve him in sending a large consignment of sample instruments, an expensive catalogue, and so on.

Will he make slight modifications as he does for his British customers (although it will be much more difficult without a face-to-face discussion)?

Will he make special instruments to order (again with the attendant difficulties)?

He may well decide to sell only a restricted range for some of the reasons mentioned or others connected with his special circumstances.

Pricing
The business is already more trouble, but the opportunity only exists largely because of labour-cost differences: what prices shall he fix to make it worth his while and permit sufficient sales to justify the agent's handling the business?

Production
Will he make for stock or order? If for order, the delivery time (including the postal delay and the formalities) may be too long; if for stock, the investment may be too large.

What would suit him best is to use the men's time, when there are no home orders, to make limited quantities for export. *His decision may probably be to treat export as a marginal factor in his production plan, useful for absorbing spare capacity and spreading expenses but otherwise too risky or in other respects undesirable.*

Finance
The agent would like him to place consignment stocks with him, but he considers:

(a) the tying up of capital unjustified;
(b) the finance risk too high.

He has therefore to relate the new investment involved to the estimated profit, and in doing so to consider, however superficially, some complex questions such as: what is profit in this context?

Since he is using spare capacity and selling more than he would otherwise sell, should he consider profit to be:

(a) only the margin after full domestic cost plus export expenses?
(b) margin (a) plus the overhead element?
(c) margin (b) plus the labour cost involved?
(d) one of the foregoing, less an element for the service of the extra capital involved and the higher finance and commercial risk?

Depending on his product, pricing and production policy decisions, he will decide either that:

(a) he should not tie up much capital in the venture, or
(b) the marginal return is so attractive that he is justified in taking more risk.

If he does, he then has to compare the competing requirements of his domestic business and the new business for fixed and working capital. In the situation we are considering, he will probably decide to give his domestic business total or virtually total priority.

Legal

The neophyte has also to consider some legal difficulties which would not arise in his ordinary business. His new business is based on a contract, a concept which in some form, if only from the lease of his premises or a bank loan, will be familiar to him, but now he has to decide under which law his contract will be interpreted; will it be British law or that of his agent's country, and if the latter, what security will it afford him?

In this first phase, having taken a decision, no doubt on expert advice, it will become one more element of risk which he will want to make some allowance for.

Administration

The complexities of packing, shipping, credit and so on will be another disagreeable surprise, and no doubt he will decide either to rely on some member of his staff who can at least discover the most essential facts or else he will use the services of a firm of export packers and shippers who will take the whole problem off his hands.

The problem may have a simple solution but, as in the case of the other aspects, he has had to consider it and take decisions between certain options.

In this first phase all or the great majority of the options taken will have been those which involve least risk and disturbance to his ordinary business; he will refuse definite commitment of any magnitude or for any long period of time. The approach is essentially opportunistic.

PHASE II – LIMITED COMMITMENT

In the second phase, opportunism is exchanged for a limited commitment. The expected profit has perhaps been realized, or is seen as sufficiently attractive to justify more effort and more involvement. The exporter may now actively seek to extend the scope of the operation, either in depth in the same country or by extending the same process to other countries, except that he will now be the initiator of the operation rather than the relatively passive participant in an operation promoted by his overseas contact.

Having adjusted his viewpoint in this way he again has a large number of decisions to take, explicitly or implicitly, although from ignorance he will in many cases adopt one course without any very detailed consideration of the alternatives. *It is a characteristic of international business that many policies, even in a sophisticated environment, are set up without consideration of anything but a small number of alternatives. This obviously arises from the enormous increase in the number of variables which arise when operations are extended to more than one country.* Moreover, many matters which can be decided competently from general knowledge and experience in the domestic market need *special* knowledge and special investigation in the overseas market. The number of variables affecting the situation increases exponentially with the number of countries, but the number of genuine *unknowns* is a far greater proportion, *since many of the factors of the domestic market which are, to some degree at least, known, become unknown in the foreign market.*

In this phase of *positive action with limited commitment*, the main options will be as follows:

Markets

It may be that the exporter will decide that the same pattern of selling can be applied to other countries, and he therefore decides to try at least one more market on the same lines. The choice between new alternative markets is not likely to be made on the basis of very sophisticated considerations, but even so it has to be made.

Consciously or instinctively at this stage he is likely to be interested in markets which seem to have some degree of familiarity, which appear to be like his domestic market and which offer stability and other features coming under the head of security. His first market may have been in an unfamiliar country, indeed it is likely to have been, since it is the grosser *differences* from his domestic market which have made his product look attractive to the foreign importer. That is, the less the products have competitors in the new market, the more attractive they will appear.

The market which represents a voluntary choice will probably present the converse conditions, ie, it will be the more attractive the more familiar it appears, but because of this it will be more difficult to penetrate. There will therefore be in many cases a subtle change in the operating conditions, of which it is unlikely that the relatively unsophisticated exporter will be aware, in the early stages at least.

His voluntary choice of markets will probably be made on a basis of the following:

Proximity – he may now consider actually visiting the export territory.

Similarity of environment – he will consider which markets are likely to be similar in conditions, ie, use of the products, and so on.

Language – this may be a relatively trivial matter, but it is in actual operating experience one of the key factors affecting choice.

Security – the choice will be largely on a basis of accumulated experience or prejudice, eg, that the Dutch are more reliable than the Italians.

He is unlikely to make any detailed first- or even second-hand exploration of the market. This will appear too difficult and in most cases he will consider it to be the function of the agent he will appoint.

Through advertisements in the trade publications, through the appropriate government department, trade promotion agencies, and so on, he will now seek to find a suitable agent with whom he can discuss the possibilities of whatever market has caught his fancy.

Products

The product strategy in this phase is likely to remain substantially the same, and probably should do so in a successful limited operation of this kind. There may be minor modifications of the products, but the range will still be a more or less limited selection from the domestic range.

Prices

The pricing strategy will be essentially the same as in the first phase, since the basic policy will still be the sale of marginal production of standard items.

There is likely to be some acceptance of a lower standard of profit, even of the notion of a contribution to overhead expense, particularly since in this second phase there has been a voluntary decision to export and a more or less voluntary choice of market, assumed to have attractive features of security, stability and more or less easy penetration.

Production

The position will be essentially the same as in Phase I: *the export commitment will be limited to marginal production capacity and no extra fixed investment will be incurred*. As the volume of business grows, however, decisions of choice between home and export customers will have to be faced. Solutions will be found involving:

(a) delays to low-priority home orders;
(b) elimination of marginal domestic customers;
(c) overtime working;
(d) perhaps some elimination of bottlenecks in production;
(e) outside purchasing of finished or semi-finished goods.

A certain tendency towards a differential quality policy may be seen in some cases during this phase. The manufacturer is conscious of the more unstable nature of the foreign business and the difficulties arising from communications and so he will tend to ensure that export orders give rise to as little trouble as possible. In spite of the fact that he still adheres to his marginal-production policy he may well tend to a higher-quality standard for his export customers.

Finance

Since he has now become committed *by choice* to an export policy he will make his financial plans, for working capital, to include export requirements. This may well involve permanent increases in capital as well as using bank credit, special export credit finance, and so on. If he uses his own working capital this will further commit him to an export policy in order to employ the funds he has available. *The employment of marginal resources on a continuous, policy-based footing must lead to this policy becoming to some extent irreversible in practice.* This is an important element in determining the next phase, as will be seen.

Legal

There will be some evolution in the handling of legal matters, particularly as regards sophistication in contracts, and consideration will probably be given to at least the more obvious aspects of *tax avoidance*.

Administration

Since he now takes an on-going (albeit limited) view of his commitment to overseas business it will be common in this phase for the manufacturer to perform some of the services himself which he has farmed out previously to specialized export-packing and -forwarding houses. He will expect to find convenience in this, a saving in time, better supervision and almost certainly a saving in cost. Some part of this packing and dispatch operation will probably result in a commitment as regards hiring specialized personnel with a knowledge of export routine, documentation, customs and shipping requirements.

This stage, therefore, of *a voluntary, positive initiative* to handle foreign business will almost inevitably result in *a longer-term time horizon and in an increasingly pervasive, complex and to some extent irreversible commitment*, although the basic policy may still be firmly to avoid fixed investment, to give the domestic market absolute preference (with the qualification mentioned), to use only marginal production capacity and to make no special products for the foreign business. Some valuable expertise will have been gained at this stage; there will be some specialization of personnel, and there will be some resources earmarked specially for foreign business. As the business grows there will be a goodwill element with a definite financial value, and so quite involuntarily there will have been capital investment (out of profits). *A capital asset will have been created in the form of goodwill in foreign markets.* The existence of some specialized facilities and personnel will constitute a further commitment. In most cases this process will be irreversible except by negligence or a policy decision. It is unlikely that the policy decision will be made since the involvement will be regarded as minimal, even when, in fact, it may be quite important.

PHASE III – LIMITED FIXED INVESTMENT

In Phase II there has been a limited policy commitment with some involuntary investment and the creation of a capital asset in the foreign market. The next phase recognizes the extent of the commitment which has been made, largely involuntarily, and becomes committed to *voluntary fixed investment*, generally in the shape of extra capacity to be used for export orders. The time horizon is lengthened, and the process of involvement is recognized consciously as being irreversible. The commitment is still limited, however, and the basic policy is one of obtaining extra profit from the foreign operations, but not relying on them for the service of capital. The number of markets served is widened and foreign business becomes a recognized function in the business.

Markets

A policy decision is taken to extend the foreign coverage. Since each new market involves some development expense, the range of decision involved becomes much more complex.

A decision must be made about the capital available for foreign-market development. A period of time longer than one year may be taken since in many cases markets will have different time horizons. It will have been realized by now in the company that the development of overseas markets, as distinct from taking advantage of adventitious demand, can be a slow and costly business. Some sort of choice between different markets has to be made, although it is extremely rare for there to be any systematic exploration of a wide range of possibilities; the staff, knowledge and resources are simply not available in this phase.

Other options covering markets are now beginning to appear as alternatives to the original method of development, ie, dependence on import agents. From the most advanced countries there may be requests for the licensing of patents and know-how, which would eventually preclude the possibility of direct export sales; there may be approaches from similar businesses for joint selling (and/or manufacturing) arrangements; there may be approaches from foreign financial interests to set up manufacturing businesses in countries where tariff or other obstacles render this desirable.

The possible choice of markets to be developed by different methods now becomes very great. The amount of expertise developed by the company in this phase, far from being adequate to the new situation, is now even less adequate. These new possibilities *have become possibilities* because of the growth of business and accompanying expertise, but they are now likely to present far more problems than the company is equipped to solve in any systematic way.

This phase then is characterized by a great increase in the range of possibilities and awareness of them, but inability to take advantage of any but a very limited number.

Products

In this phase there is likely to be some broadening of the product policy. Foreign business has been accepted as a more or less permanent feature of the company; a substantial commitment in working capital, investment and now production capacity has been made. It is therefore almost inevitable that in order to improve the economics of the operation some more major variations in the product line should be made.

The options about product policy may present themselves in the following circumstances:

In some of the markets entered new competitive products may appear, or alternatively it may be seen that attractive slices of the market could be captured with new products, either better, different or cheaper.

A commitment may have been made to development in a market on the basis of a certain product, and when substantial resources have been committed it may appear that the product is unsuitable. There will then have to be a decision as to whether the development should be abandoned or a new product manufactured.

Considerations of local market requirements in terms of:

> design
> quality
> price
> range

will all appear more pressing at this stage of development in foreign business than they have hitherto. The dangers of wrong decisions will also be greater in proportion as the commitment to foreign business has increased, particularly the multiplication of products for which orders are insufficient to make economic production runs possible.

Prices

In this essentially intermediate phase the marginal pricing policy will be increasingly followed. Development expense will be considerable and consequently a large part of the operation will only be profitable if account is taken of the contribution to overhead made by foreign sales. It will require exceptionally firm budgetary discipline to ensure that operations are profitable within a definite and acceptable time framework. This may well be more than one year in the case of new products but there will be a strong tendency for the time horizon of profitability to be indefinite, and for prices to be set too low in order to capture volume.

Production

A major distinguishing feature of this phase is the earmarking of production capacity for export business, whether in existing plant, or by increasing investment in the expansion of new plant.

The policy of using marginal production facilities has therefore been abandoned, to some extent at least. The financial decision about new capacity may still reflect the marginal-policy thinking since it is likely that there will be a reluctance to build new capacity *solely* for overseas business. The margin of capacity will in most cases be *a part of new capacity* intended for the domestic market. The reason for this will be primarily that in this phase the profitability of foreign business is likely to be lower than of domestic business, and indeed it may well be the policy that it should be, in the sense that the development of new markets will be carried out on the basis of a marginal contribution to profit. As long as the market-development policy is on this basis it will be difficult to justify investment in new facilities solely for export.

It is not uncommon, even in this intermediate phase, for there to be some involvement in manufacturing abroad. It will be a relatively limited commitment, perhaps in association with a local partner, or restricted to assembly or the final stages of manufacture (in the case, for example, of a chemical product). It will tend to be regarded as anomalous and experimental rather than the beginning of a new policy.

Finance

In this phase the financial commitment will now be quite considerable. There will be investment in domestic production resources, perhaps up to 25% of total fixed investment, and there will be a large, generally entirely unquantified investment in market development, leading to the creation of a capital asset in the form of goodwill in foreign markets. Typically, the return on all this investment will be lower than the standards required for the domestic market, since the policy of the company is still to have only a limited commitment to foreign business compared with the business as a whole.

Administration

At this stage the specialized services will now be quite important, and will have become a recognized part of company structure.

There will be an export department, the head of which may report directly to the managing director, but who in any case will rank as a senior corporate executive. There will be some specialized services on the accounting side, and the foreign business will have its own profit-and-loss account and cost-accounting facilities. The company will be basically self-sufficient in documentation and dispatch. There are now likely to be at least some personnel responsible for visiting export markets, appointing agents and supervising their performance.

The characteristic of this phase is thus a voluntary and extensive commitment to foreign business, *still regarded, however, as ancillary to the domestic business, to an extent which would prevent failure of the foreign business from seriously affecting the performance of the business as a whole. It will be recognized that the majority of medium-sized and small UK businesses are still in this phase.*

PHASE IV – MAJOR DEPENDENCE ON FOREIGN BUSINESS

When this ceases to be the case the business has entered the fourth phase; that is, when the overall performance of the company is heavily but not overwhelmingly dependent on foreign business. In this phase top management will itself devote a substantial amount of time to foreign business and will probably travel abroad extensively. There will be substantial capital investment in overseas subsidiary companies. The marginal production policy will have been entirely abandoned, and the tendency will be for foreign business to have a profit standard approximating to that of the business as a whole. If this is not the case, the corporate earnings will be reduced, since the investment in foreign business will by definition be approaching equality with domestic.

In this phase there will again be an increase in the importance and complexity of the policy decisions.

Products
The company will now face in an acute form one of the major policy decisions in international business: namely, diversification versus unification. The range of foreign markets will now be very wide; the opportunities created by greatly increased knowledge and sophistication very attractive, and there will consequently be very strong centrifugal forces tending to disintegrate central policy-making. The development of management in quasi-independent subsidiary companies will permit considerable operating decentralization. Because local conditions will differ widely and because of the smallness of many markets, products will be added to local ranges which are not made by the domestic company, and there will be a strong trend towards venturing into areas where the domestic company has no expertise.

Pricing
Pricing and profit policy will equate to those of the domestic business for the reasons given above.

Production
Production will be increasingly decentralized to subsidiary companies which, in most cases, will sell a range of products made locally by the domestic company and in some cases even by third parties, in order to spread sales costs. From the point of view of production each market will basically constitute a separate cost centre.

Finance
The company will now have reached the stage where considerable sophistication in the financial planning will be necessary. Many markets will present quite high risks to capital, either because of the danger of expropriation or because of very high rates of inflation eroding working capital, and even preventing adequate amortization of fixed assets. These are among the most important of the multiple risks, which are dealt with in detail in Chapters 6 and 7.

Administration
The typical organization pattern will now be that of an international division of the domestic company being responsible for all operating subsidiaries, whether selling or manufacturing, for agency companies, licensing etc.

The head of this division will have approximately equal status to that of the head of the domestic division. The managing director of the parent company will in many cases be chairman of the most important overseas subsidiaries.

PHASE V – NO DISTINCTION BETWEEN DOMESTIC AND FOREIGN BUSINESS – THE MULTI-NATIONAL COMPANY

The phase we have just discussed is characterized by a further commitment to foreign business to the extent that it can seriously affect the profit position of the corporation. In consequence policy decisions tend to equate to those of the domestic business on many basic aspects. In the final phase the strategy of the business is considered from a world-wide standpoint. The domestic market is considered to be only one market and the policy towards it is governed by many of the same criteria as are applied to all other markets. The world market is normally divided into areas, which may, for example, correspond to the continents. In the case of a Swiss multi-national company, the domestic operation would be considered probably as part of the European market.

In such a multi-national company, the capital may be held outside the country of origin, the shares may be quoted on all the principal stock exchanges and dividends declared in a currency not that of the country of origin.

The following is a statement by a leading US-based company:

Managing a multinational company
A multinational company has the conviction that considerations of nationality or geography should carry little weight in the selection of investment opportunities, of useful technologies, and above all of the people chosen to manage the company's affairs. ● W. R. Grace & Co. has been multinational almost since its beginning in 1854, and today one-third of sales and earnings are generated by international operations. Grace has interests in 43 countries on every major continent of the world. The largest foreign investments are in Western Europe. All principal operating groups have international production and marketing facilities. ● Under Grace's decentralized management structure, group executives have broad authority over their operations, and division executives within each group also have considerable decision-making responsibility. Group executives report to the president, who is assisted by a corporate management consisting of key officers and administrative and financial executives. The responsibility of corporate management is to make policy and audit its implementation, monitor operations, control the investment of capital funds, and evaluate the

performance of each group and of all principal executives.*

Many companies are much more dependent than W. R. Grace on foreign revenues – Nestlé about 97%, IBM over 50%, while there are the rather unusual cases of Unilever and Shell, each effectively bi-national in capital, management and domicile. They would all no doubt subscribe to that opening sentence: 'A multinational company has the conviction that considerations of nationality or geography should carry little weight in the selection of investment opportunities, of useful technologies, and above all of the people chosen to manage the company's affairs.' Neither Grace, Nestlé, IBM nor the great majority of those companies recognized as multi-national would, however, suggest that ownership and control were other than national, and indeed Mr Donner, former President of General Motors, has explicitly stated that his company could not admit of divided national ownership, other than as an investment in the United States corporation. The natural-resources companies are coming to a different view under considerable pressure and are indeed following the lead given by RTZ between ten and twenty years ago.

The theme of this chapter has largely been the self-generating and usually irreversible commitment to international business of most companies, once they are launched in that direction. In discussing the multi-national company we have come to a stage when the commitment is obviously very great and, unlike the last phase, the success or failure of the business is dependent on the world-wide business.

In many cases there is an additional commitment to international business in the form of the international *integration* of operations. This does not apply to all business, although obviously there is a strong trend in that direction, but in the case of many businesses, of which IBM, General Motors, Ford and the oil companies would be typical, there is a high degree of *international specialization of production*, operations being

* W. R. Grace & Co, 1970 Annual Report, p 9.

carried out in whichever country appears to be most appropriate. The master plan is made either at the company or regional HQ and the parts directed to whichever centre is nominated for assembly. In this way local differences of material or labour cost can be taken advantage of, and particularly there will frequently be advantages of specialization and economies of scale. This is, incidentally, one of the limited number of cases when the law of comparative advantage, mentioned in Chapter 1, does actually concern an individual enterprise.

Such arrangements are obviously dependent on a large number of conditions for their satisfactory operation, particularly exchange rates and the relative balance of costs between one country and another. Just how sensitive these conditions are to change is shown by the example of the pharmaceutical industry on pages 110–11. If things go right the multi-national company has a great advantage through international specialization; if they go wrong the disruption can be important and costly. Integration represents therefore an additional commitment to international business.

We are emphatically not concerned in this book with political issues, other than as problems with which management has to deal, but we must just note that these possibilities of integration, together with the size of many multi-national businesses, have given rise to some rather acute tensions between companies and host countries. As we have already noted, states are not highly organized internationally, and there are many gaps between the jurisdiction of national states which are not filled by international law or specific agreements. If very large multi-national corporations integrate their operations internationally they may have advantages deriving from extra-territoriality or the lack of coordination between states.

Professor Dunning indeed notes that the actions of multi-national corporations have upset the prevailing pattern of international transactions which 'had two things in common. First, each was generally undertaken independently of the other and by different economic agents. Second, most transactions were between unassociated buyers and sellers, and were concluded at market or "arm's length" prices.' * We shall have occasion to discuss some of the effects of this change in subsequent chapters.

It is beyond the scope of this chapter, or indeed of this book, to discuss in detail the operations of the multi-national corporation. Largely because of the political overtones, this is indeed an aspect of international business which has received considerable attention, to the detriment of the more general principles of international business management.

Further reading

John Fayerweather, *International Business Management – A Conceptual Framework* (McGraw-Hill Series in International Business).

Raymond Vernon, *Sovereignty at Bay – the Multinational Spread of U.S. Enterprises* (Longman).

Michael Z. Brooke and H. Lee Remmers, *The Strategy of Multinational Enterprise* (Longman).

* John H. Dunning, 'The Multinational Enterprise' (*Lloyds Bank Review*, July 1970).

CHAPTER THREE

The Nature of International Business

We have now looked very quickly at the environment in which the international businessman operates, that is to say, the external forces making operations in foreign countries, hazardous though they may be, somehow important to him. We have also looked at his reactions to these external forces, and we have tried to show the process by which, typically, he may become more and more involved in such operations.

So far, however, we have not tried to define this thing, international business; we have, as it were, tacitly assumed that we all know what it is, why and how it is different from domestic business, and what the implications may be as regards the management of these new situations.

It is readily accepted, for example, that there is such a thing as international finance; anyone having to make a payment from one country to another in 1971 must at the least buy the foreign currency, at the most obtain a number of permits, and become involved in complex formalities in perhaps two countries. The daily newspaper will speak of international liquidity, balance of payments, the state of the reserves and so on. No one doubts that there is a large corpus of knowledge involved in this subject, and a complex variety of expertise.

But international business management – is not this just an extension of business management itself? It is true that conditions in Turkey are not the same as in New York State or in London. But neither are they in Texas or California, Wales or Scotland. The differences in the market, for example, may actually be greater in a huge country like the United States than they are in a relatively homogeneous area such as Scandinavia. Here you have four countries: Norway, Sweden, Denmark and Finland, which at various times have been under the same sovereignty and which exhibit quite marked common characteristics. A great deal of the discussion about international business seems therefore to lack any strong distinguishing feature. Of course, it is important to become attuned to differences in customs and institutions but this hardly seems to justify the creation of a whole new subject.

Let us suppose that we are making a short trip by car from England to France, for business or pleasure, or from the US to Mexico. In both cases these are foreign countries, with whom we have friendly relations. They are quite close geographically; many people go to them for vacations and there is a certain familiarity about them, even to people who have never been there. They are, it is true, foreign countries but not somehow in the same category as, let us say, Brazil, the USSR or Tibet.

Nevertheless, before we start we make rather careful inquiries about visas, foreign currency, health regulations and formalities regarding the import of cars and driving regulations. We become aware that we are leaving the jurisdiction of our own country and have to comply with a whole new set of regulations, some of which seem unnecessarily different from our own. Further, before we have left our own country we have been warned about what we can or cannot do when we return; in other words, we are going to be treated by our own government, not as the returning prodigal, to be welcomed with open arms, but as a slightly suspect individual who may be attempting to break the laws of his own country when he returns. We may bring in so much of this article, but not of that: we may, we may not . . . If we have not been through this process before we wonder whether it is worth all the trouble, and we may even picture ourselves as some unhappy East African Indian family, shuttled relentlessly backwards and forwards between some foreign capital and our own country, not being acceptable anywhere.

But we assume that we surmount our fears and set off. Having passed through our own customs we survive the interrogation of the foreign customs officer, who should look on us with smiling favour as a desirable visitor to his country but in fact may take quite a different attitude.

We emerge apprehensive and, if going from England to France, apprehension is increased by the fact that if we are driving on the left-hand side of the road, as in the UK, the traffic is coming at us head on, very fast indeed. The signs, regrettably, are not in English, and our request for information from a policeman leads him to suggest that we are likely to be arrested if we proceed as we started.

In this short space of time we have acquired a good deal of knowledge useful in international business, particularly:

- We have crossed a *national frontier*.
- A new system of *fiscal, monetary and legal jurisdiction* applies.
- We have established *a new relationship with the domestic country*, and will be accountable in new areas of fiscal treatment (at least when we return).
- *Communication*, both with our former and new environment, has become more complicated.
- Practices perfectly permissible in the domestic environment are not allowed in the new one.
- We appear to be exposed to more *uncertainty* through ignorance about our environment.
- There are *risks* in the new situation not encountered in our domestic environment.
- We have to make rather drastic changes in our *frame of reference* about many subjects – rules of the road, hours of eating and a hundred and one other things, where assumptions based on our domestic conditions do not apply.

We have, in short, experienced all the major features of international business, and what we will have to say will be largely an elaboration of these basic factors.

National sovereignty

The discussion in the first chapter perhaps helped to define business, in the sense which is important to us. It may be mining, service or manufacturing, each with its own rather different characterization. The movement of men, money or goods may be involved, though not always all of them. But international? Is there a precise meaning to be given to this? Does it, as we have asked before, include dealings between widely different peoples and cultures in the same state – Ukrainians in Soviet Russia, Indians in North America or the dozens of nationalities in India? Certainly a good deal of what we have to say is relevant to such situations. Nevertheless, we are concerned here, as our example showed, with movements across national frontiers, dividing one sovereign, independent country from another; Canada and the US, the US and Mexico, England and France. It is only in these circumstances that the total international business transaction can take place. It is not, in other words, sufficient that there should exist a difference of nationality, however great; international business is concerned with transactions across boundaries of national sovereignty, and this fact is more important than any other, even where there are no major formalities to mark the crossing of the frontier, as between the US and Canada, and where the ethnic, linguistic, cultural and perhaps other differences are quite small. There are certainly greater differences between many parts of the United States than there are between the United States and Canada, but there is not *the* great difference, that of national sovereignty.

National sovereignty implies power, not absolute perhaps, but subject to few limitations, over persons and property within its frontiers. The right of *eminent domain*, as the international jurists term it, is recognized by most civilized states as limiting the rights of foreign nationals and property within the confines of another sovereign state. It would no doubt be recognized widely that the United Kingdom respects the rights of foreign nationals as far as any other state does, but nevertheless there is no doubt that if, for example in the great programmes of nationalization, important foreign assets had been involved, they would not have been treated differently from domestic assets.

Not only is this a right long recognized under international law but it has been confirmed by a formal resolution of the United Nations (Seventeenth General Assembly) entitled 'Resolution on permanent sovereignty over natural resources'. This resolution confirms the 'right of peoples and nations to permanent sovereignty over their natural wealth and resources'. Property may be expropriated 'on grounds or reasons of public utility'. It is true that it is stated that compensation should be paid in accordance with international law, but the right of expropriation is not in any way affected.

The second fact, emerging also from our story, is that the national law is the only law concerned, unless express provision has been made in some treaty or by other means for a different law to apply. International law may have something to say, but in practice few will have recourse to it. Provision may be made for difficulties in interpretation to be submitted to independent arbitration, perhaps in a third country, and this is common in cases where the philosophy of the law is very different, as between the Soviet Union, for example, and Western European countries. In earlier times it was not unusual for foreigners to claim special immunity from the laws of the country, but this implied some diminution of national sovereignty which now hardly exists in any country.

Thirdly, there is likely to be a different fiscal and monetary system, and this fact gives importance to an immense corpus of expertise which concerns taxation and foreign exchange. Because of these different systems there are likely to be major risks of capital or profits. These are important subjects in themselves which will be discussed at length.

Although there are differences in taxation and currencies in almost every state, there has been very little effective attempt to bring about agreement between states on these matters. The result is that the inconsistencies between states may mean heavy loss to the international businessman, or else an important opportunity to escape the net of both countries concerned.

No doubt in a perfect world any country intending to devalue its currency would ask all other countries not to accept money flowing out from it to escape the effects of the devaluation, but in the real world such cooperation is very limited. Individuals and companies able to forecast these movements accurately can therefore benefit themselves on the one hand and cause embarrassment to the country concerned on the other.

Similarly, since there is little harmonization of taxes, profits may be made to appear in the books of associated companies where taxation is lowest, although they may have been earned in other countries.

These are some of the more important consequences for the businessman arising out of national sovereignty; it will be seen that the lack of cooperation and standardization between states frequently acts to his advantage. Since these will be the dominant themes of our discussion we may also note the extreme complexity, inherent in these differences between states, the uncertainty and the risk, which are obviously much greater than in the domestic environment.

Cultural and environmental questions

The distinguishing feature of international business is the fact of the existence of states each with its own sovereignty, legal and monetary system, economic policy, and so on. But a good deal of our discussion will be concerned with matters where the existence of national sovereignty is not necessarily a precondition, and on our own definition, therefore, these matters would fall outside the subject. The fact is, however, that in most cases where international business is concerned there are present also a number of these other factors, particularly cultural differences and differences in communication which necessarily have to be dealt with. In many cases the difficulties are themselves exacerbated by the fact of national sovereignty as well as national identity. For example, cultural differences between Spain and Catalonia are many and important, but perhaps because there is no national sovereignty the foreigner will not be required to take notice of them. The assertion of nationalism by the Catalans will in most cases be reserved for the Spanish, and particularly the Spanish authorities.

The position is that someone who is not engaged in international business *may* have to deal with important cultural and environmental differences; someone who *is* engaged in international business will certainly have to deal with these differences. It is difficult therefore to exclude them from any book on the subject of international business management which aspires to any great practical utility.

Different cultures are concerned with religion and customs. They may be of the greatest importance: for example, the relationships between India and Pakistan, Israel and the Arab countries are more than political and in consequence harder to resolve. Although the relationships between South American countries may be equally hostile, the hostility is not rooted in cultural differences, but economic and political.

National ethos

This is largely coterminous with culture, but not entirely so. There are few cultural differences between the countries in South America, Scandinavia or the Arabian Peninsula, but the differences of national ethos are very great. These differences may arise in geography or history, or a complex mixture of factors. They are important in business relationships largely, but not exclusively, in personal matters. For example, it would be preferable not to employ a Pole as a Russian interpreter in the Soviet Union. Ostensibly there is no objection whatever, but there is a deep-seated national antipathy which can affect relationships quite seriously.

The Frame of Reference

In commenting on our little story we have used the phrase 'frame of reference' (page 60), and this is of particular importance in dealing with questions of culture, and indeed any conditions where many features of the situation are similar but where important differences may exist. Indeed, one may have two kinds of situation, the one which appears to be very different but where the important features are the same, and the converse where the situation may appear similar or even identical, but where profound differences may be concealed.

We say 'similar' or 'different', but to or from what? To or from what we are accustomed to, our past experience which will have crystallized into some pattern. It is indeed a feature of our mind and personality that all experience is processed, whether we like it or not, and generally becomes part of our subconscious stock, instantly available, like the memory of a computer, for reference and comparison with a new situation. Sometimes we are aware of this process of reference to the subconscious 'memory core', more frequently we are not. The particular pattern applied to a new situation is termed the 'frame of reference'. In the simple example with which we started the English motorist's frame of reference regarding the side of the road on which to drive in France was his experience in England where motorists (still) drive on the left. When he arrives in France he sees a road and his experience tells him to drive on the left; he is therefore greatly surprised and confused when he sees the traffic approaching head on. His previous frame of reference was limited to driving on the left and seeing traffic pass him on the right; his new frame of reference, if he survives, will be a more complex pattern of driving on the right, with traffic overtaking him on the left, and also approaching him on the left. This is a relatively simple example, but it may take him longer to learn that in Arabic countries the nod of assent in fact means the reverse, that references to 'the war' in the Southern United States may well be the Civil War of 1861–5 or that the acceptance of bribes may not be considered dishonest, because one's first duty is to one's own family where the fabric of society affords no protection or support.

The international businessman has therefore to develop an attitude of questioning towards his own frame of reference on almost every question or situation with which he may be concerned. There are now attempts to inculcate this suspension of judgement in regard to one's own frame of reference, and more will be said of this later.

Thus one of the major difficulties of international business is the need for continual changes in the frame of reference, whether it be cultural, financial, political or human. In any situation there will be well-established frames of reference relating to the same products or the same processes. It is harder to put these aside than it is to start completely *ab initio*. This carry-over of existing concepts constitutes one of the most fundamental dangers of international business.

Many companies entering new markets go through a phase of uncertainty and difficulty, perhaps even disaster, while the existing frames of reference are being adjusted to the new conditions. These frames of reference are not after all tangible things; they are concepts embodied mostly in the thinking of the company executives, often not explicit, but habits of mind rather than definite logical concepts.

The changes called for may be quite small, and this makes them harder to detect, but equally, they may be vitally important. It must be a universally applicable law that only the minimum necessary changes must be made in the existing operating philosophies and practices, because these constitute the reason for the success of the existing operation. Radical changes will be tantamount to the creation of a new business, putting the foreign business at a disadvantage, since clearly it will know less about the local environment than those native to it. If it has to evolve new products and new attitudes it will be at a double disadvantage; there are plenty of examples of failure due to this cause. This situation will apply with particular force to marketing.

Communication

It is obvious again, and illustrated in our story, that communication becomes more difficult, both internally in the new environment and externally with the domestic environment. It is not only language, (this difficulty is frequently overestimated rather than the reverse); the 'frame of reference' syndrome produces new difficulties and you get what the French describe as 'a dialogue of the deaf'.

Again, there are the purely physical difficulties of distance and the means of communication. It is frequently suggested that managing a world-wide business is now no longer any more difficult than a purely domestic one because of the enormous progress in the means of communication. The sight of so many tired individuals rushing about in aeroplanes from meeting to meeting should perhaps be sufficient to cast some doubt on this statement. It is wise to remember that communications become progressively more inadequate, not the contrary. It appears to be a law of organization that the more centralized it is, the more efficient, *provided that* the means of communication are effective.

Because of the advantages of centralization there is a constant straining of communications, always beyond the means available, and an increasing sense of frustration in large, widely diffused organizations, due to the fact that information is inadequate or initiative stultified. The study of organization has not yet reached the point where the system is designed in terms of the means of communication available.

Communication is, therefore, one of our major themes and the next chapter is devoted to this subject.

Uncertainty and risk

Our motorist does not know what to do, or what results will follow from a certain course of action; because of this uncertainty, proceeding from both ignorance and the wrong frame of reference (not, of course, the same thing), he is exposed to much greater risks than in the domestic environment.

This is obviously the case in international business also; there is generally less knowledge available than of the domestic environment – fewer people, for example, will have been exposed to conditions in the foreign country and the base of decision will in general be much narrower. To take an extreme case, in the Foreign Office (or State Department) everyone will have a view of value, no doubt, on the domestic foreign policy situation, but only the 'country desk' and a few others will have a detailed up-to-date knowledge of events in any given country.

Uncertainty and risk are therefore one of our major themes in this book.

A different balance of factors
The differences and the risks might follow a standard pattern from country to country, so that experience gained in one country would be valid for another. This is in general not so, since, while the same factors may exist, the balance may be quite different. France and Italy both have major Communist Parties, for example, and Italy, indeed, for a good many years after the war was considered by some to be a politically risky country. Investors in Italy would, however, place a number of other risks above the political one, such as the unreliability of Italian accounting and the apparent unpredictability of the tax authorities, whereas in Spain apparent order and stability have always seemed to involve much greater risks. In Brazil political instability may seem important (particularly if one is a diplomat) but to anyone operating there the erosion of working capital by inflation may seem the major management problem.

The point is that only the most intimate acquaintance with the market can assess the particular balance of factors making for success or failure, security or loss.

Relationship with the host country
Even in our highly simplified example the visitor's relationship with the country he has entered has already created problems: the customs, police and so on. In the world of business, particularly if the 'visitor' is a foreign company established as a legal entity, ie, as some form of limited company especially, then the problems it encounters have almost a direct relationship to its size and importance.

The first problem arises naturally from its ambiguous position: it is supposed to be a local legal entity, whereas in fact the directors may have little or no real power and its actions may be governed by decisions taken in some other country. Even when these actions are perfectly normal and legal they may well excite resentment, as in the case of lay-offs made in France in the sixties by certain US companies. It is somehow suspected that this may be in the interests of some other country rather than the one in which the trouble occurs, and the 'absentee landlord' syndrome comes into play.

Then there are, of course, rather definite facts, eg, profits can be siphoned off in various ways, and thus escape the local tax collector. A frequent complaint is that no local personnel are trained and that the know-how of the foreign firm does not add to the local stock of knowledge; that the capital has been built up out of profits made locally, and little foreign exchange has been contributed.

If there is great disparity between the power of the 'visitor' and the host country, then the conflicts may well become acute. A symptom of these attitudes was the appearance in the late sixties of a book called *The American Challenge* by J. J. Servan-Schreiber.

The subject is a large and complex one, but it may be mentioned that the difficulties are greatly increased in many countries by the absence of any foreign-investment law. It is noteworthy, as has been remarked, for example, that in Canada, in spite of the fact that about 50% of all industry is foreign-controlled, and that there is much complaint and anxiety about this situation, nevertheless there is no government policy embodied in a foreign-investment law. Laws are, of course, subject to change with changes of government, but they have assisted in a number of cases in clarifying the relationship between 'host' and 'visitor' and consequently in attracting foreign investment.

Relationship with the 'domestic' country
It is frequently forgotten that, as we showed in our example, the relationship of the traveller to his own country is changed

by the fact of going abroad. In terms of business this relationship is changed principally because of two factors, namely foreign exchange and taxation.

Few governments are indifferent to movements of foreign exchange, and in many cases these movements are regulated by elaborate administrative ordinances. Even the United States has not been exempt from balance of payments difficulties and has had to hinder or restrict the flow of funds abroad. Similarly, many governments take an interest in the holdings of foreign exchange even when these are outside the domestic country.

Nearly all governments take an interest in the foreign earnings of their nationals from the point of view of tax, and restrictions have tended to become tighter in this respect, even when control over capital movements may have been relaxed.

In this somewhat restrictive world of the seventies, therefore, the international businessman tends to be like our returning traveller, rather less of a prodigal son returning to the fold than an object of suspicion, presumed guilty until proved innocent of offences against many and complex laws and regulations.

Decision complexity

This is the third of our main themes, the other two being risk (including uncertainty) and communication.

The affairs of any great corporation trading only within the domestic market are extremely complex. The practices in any one plant or unit of the organization will have repercussions on the others; no decision, whether of buying or selling, can be made without considering the financial implications. We wish to suggest, however, that in international business there is a new dimension in differences, a new complexity in decision making such that it is not only of a different order but even of a different kind.

In the first place, the differences between the environment of the foreign operation will be very different from the domestic, more so no doubt than the most extreme differences in the home market. Then there will probably be differences of scale and even kind between the operations of the domestic business and the foreign operation. Then the complexities of laws, finance, nationalities and communications, which we have mentioned. No one situation can be considered in isolation; what is done in Mexico may well have repercussions on France or Birmingham or Detroit. These differences make the increase in decision complexity, as each new territory is added, of an exponential rather than a linear order.

Centrifugal forces and sub-optimization

If one imagines the headquarters as the centre and the various foreign operations as the periphery, then there will be various forces pulling at the foreign operations and other forces pulling against the centre. One must obviously not push the physical analogy too far but it may be convenient to speak of the latter forces as 'centrifugal'.

Let us suppose that a foreign unit has started as a completely independent organization, and has been acquired by the domestic operation as a useful base on which to build, a common enough situation. Given that the business has been acquired, not purely as an investment but as an extension of the domestic business, then the latter will seek to obtain control of its operations. In the first place, if the domestic business is a public corporation it will need to ensure that the accounts of its new acquisition are properly audited, so that the figures can be accepted by the auditors of the now parent company. Secondly, it may well require that the accounts be audited by the local branch or correspondent of the auditors of the parent company. This is not always necessary, but it frequently proves more convenient.

Then the parent company will have an established budgeting and planning procedure, and a system of reporting generally at monthly intervals, but sometimes more frequently. The new acquisition must be integrated into this system, and at an early stage it will no doubt receive a bulky volume, addressed to the comptroller or chief accountant, laying down detailed procedures for budgeting and reporting. There will probably be a visit from a member of the accounts staff of the parent company. Then there will be president-to-president communications at first; later the president of the subsidiary tends to find that he is reporting further down the hierarchy of the parent.

The controls gradually become more complex until the parent company feels that it has established sufficient control first for its own reporting purposes and secondly to ensure that nothing is likely to go badly wrong without some advance warning. Generally, if the business has been prosperous and well managed, more positive direction about changes in the structural nature of the company's activities will be postponed until later.

Even a modest measure of control tends to set up opposite reactions, and there will almost invariably be resistance, passive or active, to the more detailed controls. The business will have its own dynamic and its own plans; these may have been made before its acquisition and may well carry the business off on a course not particularly desired by the parent company. Friction about plans will appear, and the nationalism of the subsidiary company may well become opposed to the nationalism of the parent.

These are common, indeed normal, experiences and they will tend to reduce effective control from the centre, whatever the detailed controls may be. There will in other words be a constant and pervasive tendency for the central policy of the headquarters to become attenuated, changed in emphasis, and even effectively disintegrated. Paradoxically, the better managed it is and the more successful, the more this trend is likely to be marked.

This is, of course, not a phenomenon peculiar to international business, but it is certainly one to which international business is particularly exposed, since it is to a large extent a function of communication. This question will not be fully explored in this book, since this would involve a detailed consideration of organizational concepts, a subject which will be reserved for the following volume.

It is sufficient to note here that this tendency to *sub-optimization* of policies is one which every international business experiences in varying degrees. If it is allowed to go too far it may mean that the specific expertise of the parent company is not used, and with the handicap of controls and ineffective communications the business may actually suffer seriously from the association with the parent company.

The distinguishing features of international business

We may now summarize these various features which are either peculiar to international business, or are found in a degree so much greater than normal in the domestic environment that they cannot be neglected in practice.

- The transmission of resources across boundaries of national sovereignty.

- The regulation by governments of such transmission.

- Changed relations with the domestic government.

- Relations with the host society and government.

- The incomplete nature of inter-government regulation; extra-territoriality.

- Major problems of communication, both internal and external.

- An exponential increase in the number of variables which management has to deal with at the centre; every discussion of international business involving by definition consideration of the effects on the domestic operation *and* the situation in the overseas market.

- A different dimension of risk in each case.

- A unique balance of factors in each case making for success or failure.

- Centrifugal forces pulling against the centre and tending to fragment policy – the dilemma of diversification and unification; non-congruence of goals of management.

- Tendency to sub-optimization.

The implications for management
These are largely the subject of the book, so we will only indicate here the most important aspects:

- *The increase in the number of variables, ie, decision complexity*, is such an important feature of international business that it must be recognized as a major problem and handled accordingly. A policy decision will have to be taken regarding the number of situations which can be handled with the resources available, ie, *a programme of priorities*. The *organization* will have to be redesigned to take care of a more complex situation.

- The *risk factor*, which is a function of lack of knowledge of local situation and decision complexity, has to be the subject of special policies and actions. Any company having an important commitment to international business will establish a *risk policy* and will set up *planning and forecasting mechanisms* designed to reduce uncertainty and minimize risk.

- *Communication* is recognized as one of the vital areas and *organization, personnel policies and public relations* particularly will reflect this importance.

- Relations with governments and government policies, domestic and foreign, as well as *extra-territoriality*, will be the subject of special study; financial management particularly will be competent to deal with the vital fiscal and monetary aspects of governmental policies.

- The need for adaptation to new *frames of reference* will be specifically recognized by *training of staff* and *mechanisms* for cross-checking of research findings and recommended policies.

● The *tendency to sub-optimization* and fragmentation of policies will be countered by the *involvement of staff at the periphery* in policy making; *adequate explanation and liaison arrangements* and a continual re-examination of *the locus of decision*, ie, what decisions on what subjects should be made where.

These are the basic elements of international business management; the successful international company is not therefore merely a company which has been successful in its domestic market and decides to go into international business. If it does so without specific and special policies and without properly trained personnel the chances are that it will fail, at least until it has bought sufficient expertise at the price of failure.

CHAPTER FOUR

Communication

It will be readily accepted that communication is extremely important in international business management. The most obvious example is the frequent need to use foreign languages, with all the inconvenience, annoyance and possibility of misunderstanding that this can give rise to. But this is not the most important aspect of an extremely complex and pervasive problem; indeed, a knowledge of foreign languages, while frequently valuable, is rated fairly low in most cases in the hierarchy of skills for overseas executives.

Communication is indeed essential to organization itself. Obviously two or more people who are trying to accomplish some common task cannot do so effectively unless they can agree on some plan for cooperation, and that implies the ability to communicate with each other. There are two elements in any form of communication – the message and the means of transmitting it. In the case of two or three people in a group the means of communication may be the voice or even a sign; organization itself then consists of the message, the means of communicating it and the purpose for which the organization exists.*

This is only another way of saying that organization is a system. Jack Morton of the Bell Telephone Laboratories – a man very much concerned with some of the most important developments in modern communication, including the transistor and Telstar – described a system in these words:

A system is an integrated assembly of specialized parts acting together for a common purpose. The components of a

* Avison Wormald, 'Men and Machines – a new theory of organization', *Times Review of Industry and Technology*, Sept 1965.

system may be physical particles in an atom or electronic components in a computer; they may be biological cells in a plant or animal; they may also be specialized ideas and knowledge in a philosophical system. But whatever the components, an assembly of specialized parts or functions, acting cooperatively for a common purpose, is generic to the idea of any system.

The pattern always is one of a group of entities, each having a specialized, essential function. But each is dependent for its system effectiveness upon its couplings to the system's other parts and the external world. Each entity of the system receives information or energy from its neighbors and from the system's environment; each entity processes this information or energy in its specialized way and sends its outputs to the rest of the system and to the external world.

We must think of every system as part of some larger system – as part of its environment – for only in its interactions with its environment are the system's inputs and outputs defined. For example, a computer must have access to its program, its data, and its user; an animal cannot be divorced from its food supply; a plant needs soil, water, and solar radiation; an industrial organization needs raw material, capital, and consumer markets – and must also have access to people and knowledge 'markets'! The 'identity' of a system – its purpose – is defined by its relation to its environment.

When we think of a system, we must place equal emphasis on purpose, parts, and the communications links and couplings between the parts. Without parts, there is no system; with parts and no couplings between the parts, there is still no system; and with parts and no purpose, there is no coupling and no system! Specialized *parts*, *couplings* and *purpose* are the three characteristics which define every system.

The specialized parts of any system (and the system and its environment) are coupled together through an exchange of information or energy.*

* J. A. Morton, *Organizing for Innovation* (McGraw-Hill Book Company, 1971), pp 12–13.

Of course, in the ordinary sense the word organization is used to describe a group of people – the staff and work people – and quite frequently implies also the factories and even the intangible property of the firm, such as know-how, designs, and so on. An industrial firm is some kind of entity and a word is needed to describe it, but perhaps 'firm' or 'enterprise' is better than 'organization'. However, there is felt by most people to be some essential element which holds the whole thing together in an environment which constantly threatens its existence, and that is something intangible which has come to be called 'organization'. Descriptions of exactly what this thing is have not been very satisfactory; they have either been too crudely physical, based on engineering analogies with simple machines, or else so metaphysical that they seem more or less meaningless. Chester Barnard, a communications engineer by training, came near to a satisfactory definition in his analogies with an electrical field, but he was still handicapped by the inability to separate the essential concept from the people and the physical trappings which went with it. In our day, especially with the advent of the computer, it is easier, too easy perhaps, to see people as only one means of accomplishing a task.

People are no longer looked on as essential elements in an organization, but few if any organizations exist without them, and no sensible theory can leave them on one side. If we look on an organization as a completely abstract entity, that is, a set of messages programmed in sequence to serve a particular purpose – let us say a set of instructions for playing a game of chess, the object of which is to checkmate the king – then people, if they exist in the organization, are there to originate, send and receive the messages, and act on them.

The game of chess we mentioned might be played by a computer, and as is now well known computers can be programmed to play quite sophisticated chess; messages come in to the computer giving the necessary information about the opponent's moves, the computer searches in its memory for analogous situations, finds the one which seems the optimum in terms of the situation on the board and makes its move. It is hard to deny to this complex process the title of 'organization'.

But people are involved somewhere, no doubt; in programming the game, perhaps monitoring it, like the men at the Houston space centre, for malfunctioning, and these men are animated by common purposes and communicate together to achieve these purposes.

But they are also people with lives and needs of their own, and so they form a social system, and within the large social system there are myriads of smaller social systems, formed sometimes on a fairly permanent basis by like-minded people, sometimes quite evanescent, like a group discussing some problem for a moment and in doing so having a common purpose, however transient, and exchanging messages in order to achieve it.

The ostensible purpose of this group of people is to accomplish some task, generally not related at all to their own needs and lives – perhaps to get the spacecraft to the moon. The whole task, no doubt, might be accomplished by one superman and a bank of computers, like some immensely sophisticated electric generating station, where a man is hard to find. Most tasks in our world are too complex for this, and so numbers of people are involved, and as soon as there is more than one we have a social system to deal with; if it is a man and a woman it will probably be a complicated one with drives of its own and perhaps tending to override the ostensible function of the organization.

The point is that the social systems are organizations themselves, that is, sequences of messages for particular purposes, and usually they will have little to do with the ostensible purpose of the *work* organization. Of course, the more they concentrate on the latter and the less on their own social purposes, the quicker the desired *work* purpose is likely to be achieved. Therefore, work organizations try to eliminate the extraneous purposes of the social organizations as far as they can, or to make them coincide with the purposes of the work organization.

This is the picture that Chester Barnard had in his imagination, but he had difficulty in conceiving of the organization without people or, at least, in seeing that the people only existed to produce and receive messages, conveying information about the environment ('feed-back'), and discussing how to achieve the purpose, or one of the myriads of sub-purposes into which it is normally broken down in a complex organization. The social organization existed merely as a means of keeping the people together and frequently, in so far as its purposes were different from those of the work organization, only as a necessary evil.

The system is very inefficient in any circumstances but much more so in international business, for the most obvious reasons; what is more, these difficulties are both on the work organization, ie, the abstract level, and on the people level, where the problems of social organization are obviously extremely complex.

This view of the nature of organization enables us incidentally to produce a more general theory embracing management, forecasting and planning. All these matters offer special difficulties in international business, so we may have here a useful analytical tool with which to take them apart and display their basic mode of operation.

In any consideration of this subject the basic principles are therefore the following:

1. The communications system
- *The purpose of the communications*, divided into main purpose and many sub-purposes.

- *The content of the communications*, ie, the subject matter.

- *The means of communication*, whether radio or language, signs or speech (and including the obstacles to communication).

2. The social system
People are essential to the communications system (or organization) and constitute a communications system of their own, whose purpose is intended to be the proper

functioning of the organization/communications system. It will have other purposes, of course, some of which have nothing to do with the organization purpose, and will be more or less efficient according to the extent to which these purposes are convergent with or divergent from the organization purpose.

We have distinguished two elements in the communications nexus, namely:

the content or message;
the means of communication.

It can be said that the efficiency of any organization (other things being equal) is proportional to the efficiency of *the means of communication*, so that where distance and language play such an important part, clearly the means of communication have a special importance as compared with those in the domestic business.

Indeed, in international business the difficulties and inefficiencies of communication are of a different order altogether from those of a national business. In very large countries distance *can* be a problem; in international business it almost always is. In large countries, again, different languages, cultures and even nationalisms can be barriers to communication; in international business they are almost always barriers.

Since in talking about business organization we are talking about organizations of people, we will also be considering the social system aspect of organization which obviously has special features in international business.

We believe that the problems of international business are to a large extent problems of communication, and for this reason we have thought it important to analyse the role of communications in organization, and we cannot conclude this part of the discussion better than by quoting from a recent and exceptionally perceptive study of an actual situation, the Japanese/US textile negotiations:

The 'age of communications' is a phrase one often hears as being characteristic of the contemporary world. Man today is exposed to enormous quantities of information on a scale that has no parallel in human history. Accordingly, the problem of communication in a society with sophisticated technology is qualitatively different from the problem of communications in earlier eras.

Particularly in international communications where information must be transmitted about different political, economic and social structures, through different cultures and often through different languages, the problem of transmitting accurate information is enormous. While in previous centuries a major problem in international communication was the scarcity of information, a major problem today is an over-abundance of information. The problem is not simply to find out what is going on but to communicate accurately the significance of what is going on.

The problem is compounded because of the speed with which modern technology fosters communication. The instant relay of information has greatly decreased the time-span between the input of information into a communications network, its reception and subsequent behaviour. Consequently, there is often little time to check the accuracy of information before making a response. The ability to communicate instantly has increased the dangers of miscalculation as the response to each input of information is fed back into the communications network and modifies subsequent behaviour.

For Japan and the United States the problem of communicating accurate information has particularly difficult aspects. On the most basic level of language there are enormous problems. There are few Americans who can communicate effectively in Japanese and too few Japanese who have an adequate command of English. Differences in the political and social structures of the two countries raise complex problems of interpretation. Furthermore, significantly large sectors of the public in the two countries have stereotyped views of the other that make the accurate evaluation of information received especially difficult.*

Of course, communications cannot alter fundamental opposition of interests, whether personal or public, and these inevitably exist; but most organizations suffer far more from misunderstandings than they do from fundamental opposition of interests. It is therefore worth while looking at all these matters in detail to see what remedies may be applied.

ENVIRONMENTAL CONDITIONS AFFECTING COMMUNICATIONS

Distance

Physical distance, even with the great and continuing improvement in communications of all kinds, is not a negligible problem in the world-wide business. Indeed, because communications have improved, organization has been adapted to them, and whereas only a few years ago, in the further countries at least, it was necessary to 'trust the man on the spot', now there is a constant straining in most organizations for more information and more control, just because they have become possible to a much greater extent. Communications are, therefore, always inadequate and, paradoxically, the more they improve the more inadequate they become. We believe that it is a fundamental law of organization that the most centralized organization is the most efficient, provided that the means of communication are efficient. The human organism, with its specialized central nervous system and brain, is greatly superior to less organized systems. Organization is, therefore, continually striving to become more centralized and is always straining the possibilities of communication. The most highly centralized world organization is the diplomatic organization of a world power, in instant communication by its own private radio circuits with its

* Gerald L. Curtis, 'The Textile Negotiations – a Failure to Communicate', *Columbia Journal of World Business*, Vol VI, No 1, Jan–Feb 1971.

ministry of foreign affairs. The most important matters have to be allocated the most efficient means of communication, such as the 'hot' line between the President's office in Washington and the Kremlin.

It is perhaps wise to assume that distance has not yet been annihilated and that therefore the trend to centralization should be allowed to proceed only as far as communications, particularly with the limitation of physical distance, permit. The alternative is in many cases the compromise which sheer size obliged General Motors to invent, namely the centralization of policy and the decentralization of operations. The advances in data processing, model building and forecasting of all kinds have improved the possibilities of long-range planning to a point where it is a major factor in policy planning. The more precise, detailed and long-term the planning, the less the need for intervention in day-to-day operations. Dr Max Gloor of Nestlé says:

> Now, control is exercised in the first place through an elaborate system of budgeting. . . .
>
> Parallel to the yearly planning, a long-term forecasting system exists with which we have experimented for more than 10 years. Once it is solidly established – and we think we have reached that stage now – it will actually be the basic planning into which the yearly plans will have to be integrated.*

And in RTZ:

> While all our headquarters departments, such as Tax, Legal, etc, are obviously so essential, we regard our Group Planning Department, which includes long-range planning and economic forecasting, as having a key function in our headquarters.†

* Dr Max Gloor, 'Policies and Practices at Nestlé Alimentana S.A.'
† Roy W. Wright, *The Policies and Practices of the Rio Tinto Zinc Corporation Ltd.*

An interesting sidelight on the planning/distance nexus is given by the same writer, Mr Roy Wright, in the following passage:

> When these negotiations for very large contracts take place we have present with us two or three members of the planning department who, before leaving London or the local national headquarters, have prepared a computer programme, so that during negotiations we are able to get rapid answers to problems that may be thrown up during the talks. For instance, there may be a contract comprising different types of the same material produced from a mine (such as an iron ore mine) and variations in the quantity, price or specification of each type within the total contract obviously affect the overall equation of production costs and profitability.*

The larger and more complex the organization and the greater the difficulties of communication, the more important are detailed, accurate and long-range plans. Clearly, however, there must be much personal contact, and this is a matter on which some companies have developed at least a philosophy, if not a policy. Meetings in particular are necessary:

● To examine matters in detail with the assistance of supporting staffs. They will therefore be at HQ or in the foreign country according to the nature of the talks – top policy being generally at HQ and more detailed discussions in the foreign country, so that more local expert advice may be at hand.

● To 'get the feel of the situation', which may be important in spite of all the paperwork.

● To avoid the development of a 'we and they' mentality, one of the most important barriers to communication which has to be countered by a variety of means, by the indoctrination

---

* Roy W. Wright, op cit.

of personnel, or rotation between HQ and the territories. Mr Roy Wright is interesting on this subject:

The national plans are prepared on the spot by the local teams and then welded together into a Group plan. When the national plans have been agreed on by the local management, they are reviewed by the Group Planning Department in London. We then have a series of meetings in each country when Val Duncan or I, together with the London Executive Directors concerned, discuss in detail the plan with the local team under the chairmanship of the local Chairman. We join those meetings with the emphasis being on our membership of the local team rather than as London Directors.

When all the national plans are settled we then have an annual top-level Group conference where the Chairman and two or three senior Directors from each national company meet with us to analyse the Group plan and the impact on it of their national plan. We change the venue of this conference each year, moving to Toronto, Melbourne, London or Johannesburg. We keep the number attending to a total of, say, about 12, calling in the experts and planners from headquarters and from each country as required. The organization of these meetings is undertaken by the local planning department and each country in turn shows its paces in setting up the meeting and providing all the necessary services. Such a small conference (referred to throughout the Group as 'the Summit Meeting') makes the Group a reality to each national company and the free interchange of thinking, criticism and ideas is quite an experience. We are then all thinking in terms of the total Group and not just as nationals.*

And he terminates his account with this paragraph:

This then is the picture of how RTZ operates around the world. If I had to lay stress on any one particular aspect, I

* Roy W. Wright, op cit.

would choose the constant high-level communication by personal contact which we maintain with our overseas national companies and operating companies. Although communication by telex and telephone plays a very important part in our Group, it cannot replace the face-to-face discussion, which avoids all ambiguity and not only allows firm decisions to be taken jointly and without delay, but binds us together as part of a world team.*

Distance therefore is both a physical fact and a psychological phenomenon of great importance. In the case of the latter it is perhaps wiser to recognize the limitation of the means of communication and to provide at both ends means to strengthen the relatively weak and infrequent signals. In both aspects the situation is assisted by intermediaries, whether they are 'country' desks at HQ or regional managers at intermediate points geographically (or, as in the case of Nestlé, stationed at HQ). Strong regional managers with a special knowledge of, and interest in, particular territories are very valuable in interpreting both sides and translating messages (we are not of course referring to foreign languages) received or to be sent into the terms most likely to convey the meaning intended.

Coordination is essentially this function of scrutinizing the two-way flow of messages, strengthening those which are becoming weakened in the process of transmission or submerged in the multitude, eliminating those which will cause confusion and generally ensuring that the flow does contribute to the objectives of the organization. Physical distance is frequently the strongest factor in weakening and confusing the message flow.

Nationalism

Nationality, culture and language are overlapping concepts but they are not coterminous. Nations largely form the states of today, the 'nation state', but there are nations which have no

* Roy W. Wright, op cit.

state, such as the Eskimos or the American Indians; and there are states which contain many different nations, such as India or the Soviet Union. Neither are culture and nationality coterminous; the Basques and the Scots have a very distinctive culture but they are hardly nations. Language has been the principal determining factor in drawing many national boundaries, and language and culture are often closely associated, language being the principal vehicle of advanced cultures, but again they are neither synonymous nor coterminous.

Nationality, and still more nationalism, are important in communications chiefly because of the barriers to rational understanding which are created by political attitudes both in the 'domestic' country and the 'host' country. We have quoted Dr Curtis earlier and his reference to 'stereotypes' which hinder understanding. The political attitudes on both sides greatly hinder communications between the United States and Latin America; between Great Britain and South Africa, and so on. It has nevertheless proved possible to establish working relationships between organizations concerned with very different national attitudes, such as the Soviet Union and the UK. A recognition of the differences is required, and perhaps this is easiest to achieve where they are so marked, and probably so irreconcilable. The hardest to reconcile are the love-hate, ambivalent relationships between competing nationalisms.

The extractive industries, petroleum and mining, face this type of difficulty in a particularly acute form because they are in fact removing physical wealth from the soil of the host country. As Mr Roy Wright says:

You must remember that, when we open a mine, the local population sees us literally and physically removing wealth from the ground and shipping it out of the country and this can very easily arouse emotional and political controversies even in the most advanced countries. We do not think it reasonable or even practical to ignore these national feelings however much we can point to the development, the wealth and the employment we are creating for the particular country.*

He goes on to say how in the case of RTZ this delicate problem is dealt with – as far as it can be dealt with:

> When we start in a new territory, we always discuss with the local government our general philosophy and explain in depth how we shall proceed, so that there can be no misunderstanding. Often we seek modifications to existing tax or royalty laws, and occasionally, in those countries where large-scale mining has not previously been known, we help draft new legislation to put that particular country on a par with other important mining countries. This we accept as a major responsibility because governments come and go but we cannot move our mine, so the mining tax laws we ask for must not only be fair and sensible to the host country and to us, but must be understood to be so by reasonable politicians of all shades and by the population generally. If we are welcomed by the government, we set up a 100% owned company and then form below that another company known as the local national company.†

Inevitably, there are cases when it is not a failure of communications which is involved but a clash of interests, and then the employee of the subsidiary company must sacrifice his own national feelings to the overall interest of his company:

> . . . in addition to the loyalty to his country he must develop a loyalty to the international company: the two may sometimes come in conflict, for instance in matters relating to transfer of profits at a time of stress on the balance of payments, or in questions such as whether a company should have local shareholders; or in export matters, considering the obvious tendency of the international company to draw

* Roy W. Wright, op cit.
† Roy W. Wright, op cit.

its export requirements from the cheapest available source. It is granted that such conflict can also occur within a national company, but allegiance to a foreign company certainly has a particular touch of its own.*

It may sometimes seem that an easy solution to some of the problems can be found in the appointment of a national of the country concerned who has been thoroughly indoctrinated in the country of origin of the HQ company. There is frequently, for example, a feeling that an Italian American or Dutch American will prove an ideal manager for an American company in Italy or Holland respectively. A great deal obviously depends on the individual but in many cases his knowledge of the local scene and the language is offset by other factors. He sees his country of origin as inferior, is anxious to show his American superiors that he is 100% American, while on the other side he is seen from an ambivalent viewpoint of envy on the one hand and dislike on the other. He is probably largely 'deculturized', and certainly no longer shares the political and national aspirations of his former fellow-countrymen, which is almost the definition of a traitor. On the whole, there are probably far more failures than successes with this type of appointment.

Culture

What is culture? In the wide sense with which we are concerned here it is not easily definable. Perhaps we may find help with the anthropologists:

> The culture of people comprises the complete structure of ideas, beliefs, morals, laws, language and all the tools, weapons, machines and other devices which they employ to cope with their lives on this planet. This culture they receive from their parents, and Lowie has defined it as 'social tradition'.†

* Dr Max Gloor, op cit.
† J. Manchip White, *Anthropology* (Teach Yourself Books), p 88.

The matter is certainly not made easier by the fact that culture is not homogeneous in even the most ancient and well-established social and national groups. In Britain there is certainly a deep-rooted and distinctive culture, but the popular culture of daily life is greatly influenced by American and even cosmopolitan cultures. The business culture of the entire world is obviously strongly influenced by American theory and practice.

Culture is both tenacious and pervasive, influencing the business enterprise in every facet of its activity, in the relationships between the HQ and the foreign subsidiary, between the expatriates in the subsidiary and their native-born staffs, between the company as a whole and the buyers of its goods and the providers of its services. It is not even necessary that there should be any antipathy, although there frequently will be, because the foreign body will be felt as an irritant, like a speck of dust in the eye; it is sufficient that it should be different.

In international business everyone has had experience of these cultural clashes. A typical case is of a well-known Dutch business acquired by a major American conglomerate. The business was one of the oldest in the world in its particular trade and had had at one time a world-wide reputation. In the negotiations which eventually led to the acquisition, both sides, as is customary in a courtship of this kind, had been on their best behaviour. The emphasis had been on how well they were fitted to live together, not on how difficult it was going to be; on how much they had to give each other, not on how difficult it would be for one to give and for the other to receive.

The acquisition followed the usual course. The accountants came from New York to re-shape the accounting system so that it could provide the figures needed for the consolidated accounts of the parent and for the budgets and control figures which were assumed to be part of the way of life of the Dutch company, but which in fact were not. The usual legalistic rituals were enacted, so that representatives of the American company could become members of the Board of the Dutch company. A Dutch American was introduced into the situation as the interpreter of the American way of life to the Dutch management.

All this seemed straightforward enough. The American company had had a long tradition of international business, principally, however, in South America and the UK, and was persuaded that it understood how to do business in foreign countries. There was a good deal of truth in this belief, particularly in the area of taxation, insurance against risk in the negotiations, and the ability to recruit and employ foreign nationals. There existed, however, certain stereotypes about different kinds of European and how they behaved which had little basis in fact. It was supposed that the mentality, particularly in business, of the Dutch was more akin to the American than other European nationalities and that, for historical reasons, there was a basic rapport. Even if this was so, it was not a help to the process of assimilation because the Dutch company did not readily accept that they were similar but more backward. They happened to live in a small country, the acquirers in a large country.

The Americans for their part had conducted the negotiations and the subsequent meetings in the manner befitting an American business of the highest reputation and integrity. What had been said was intended, but intended in the context of American ways. If, for example, the Dutch executives who were managing the business did not prove as good as both sides hoped and assumed, they would quickly be replaced, with generous compensation, of course, but not too much time would be lost in trying to make the best of a bad job or waiting to see whether things might change for the better. Certainly, it did not occur to the Americans that the Dutch might have understood anything else. In America the attitude of the American company would have seemed not just normal, but liberal and understanding.

These differences in attitudes, so fundamental that neither side could realize that they existed, polarized around particular acts and persons, but these were the symptoms, not the causes.

The fact that accountants could appear overnight, establish themselves in offices and make direct contact with their counterparts in the Dutch organization seemed to the Dutch management a direct affront to their position, and a flouting of the hierarchical principle fundamental to the Dutch method of operation. There might be no objection to the accountants, but they should be responsible to the Dutch management, who should provide them with the information they needed.

Then the Board: in the United States and Anglo-Saxon countries generally the Board *is* the management of the business; it may, as most Memoranda and Articles recite, appoint one or more of its members to manage the business on its behalf, but it is essentially responsible, legally and by custom, for management to whatever extent it may think fit. The Dutch Board, on the other hand, existed to supervise the actions of the managers, who were appointed by the shareholders, were responsible to them and could only be removed by them. So although the Board in this particular case might be synonymous with the shareholders, since the company was a wholly-owned subsidiary, the managers had not seen the appointment of the American representatives as a direct measure of policy and operating control but merely as the appointment of observers who would report to the American shareholder on the conduct of the business by the managers. To the Americans the Board was the effective instrument of control and indeed its constitution and use represented in their minds a considerable concession to local custom and pride, since a more normal method of effective control would have been by direct instruction to the managers.

There was therefore a sharp conflict of cultures on several levels – the national level, the personal level and the business culture level. Such conflicts have been the rule rather than the exception in the relations of American business with Europe. More recently both sides have become aware of the deep differences existing between even the best-disposed representatives of either side, and this mutual awareness has made for a more realistic approach to the situation.

With characteristic thoroughness American management teachers have analysed the phenomenon, isolated elements which can be taught and indeed made it part of the general corpus of management knowledge; 'culture shock' and methods of adaptation to greatly different cultures are now well recognized features of the international personnel manager's intellectual equipment. To use Professor Perlmutter's phraseology, Americans are now taught to abandon their 'ethnocentric' posture and to become 'polycentric' or perhaps even 'geocentric'.

The first feature in this process is teaching the awareness that one's own attitudes to the world and to life are only one set of attitudes, no more self-consistent or logically desirable than those of other civilized peoples. The second stage is awareness and analysis of other types of behaviour, and then recognition of their equal validity with one's own. This does not imply in any way adopting, except as a matter of convenience, the way of life of other people, but considering them as valid as, if different from, one's own. It is an attitude primarily of respect.

Recognition of these differences does not, unfortunately, remove them. It can prevent a great deal of needless irritation, perhaps leading to opposition on either side, but many of the basic factors in the situation will be irreconcilable. The American businessman's factual, quantitative orientation cannot be reconciled with the old-style European businessman's rhetorical, speech-making approach. The most that can be done is to build up a body of executives in the host country who either are or can be made into the same mould as their masters. Every nation is made up of highly heterogeneous elements and some people are more open to influence than others: it is on these elements in the situation that the new structure must be built. The recognition and acceptance of different cultural patterns will nevertheless have been extremely important in this process of rapprochement. First, it will have put both sides on their guard against believing that the other is exactly as they are, with only some superficial quirks dividing them. Secondly, it will have helped to smooth over that difficult period when it is recognized that there are considerable *real* difficulties which, however, are still regarded as unnecessary and undesirable. Thirdly, an atmosphere of trust will be possible, when a true marriage of minds can be planned and prepared. Key positions, where the practices and attitudes of the invader must be adopted, will be filled by those who can adapt themselves or who already have the necessary qualities, those more culturally intractable being pushed out round the periphery where they are in contact with their own people. By a careful analysis of the requirements of the situation the minimum disruption will be produced.

Important questions which may be asked about individuals are:

Do the needs of the job require him to be more native oriented or owner/culture oriented?

Is his native/culture orientation merely an irritation or is it really a handicap?

What is the minimum degree of owner/culture orientation which the business must have?

Where is owner/culture orientation likely to be a positive disadvantage?

It is quite easy to find men who are basically unacceptable to either side, through an ambivalent cultural attitude. The American who appears too English, the Englishman who is too French – these produce a slight feeling of unease on both sides. Perhaps more understanding of the other culture is called for, rather than imitation.

If in the case of our Dutch illustration there had been a conscious and specific awareness of the differences both in national and business cultures there could have been a period of conscious preparation on both sides. Key members of the staff would have been carefully prepared for the shock of the first real encounters and undoubtedly they would have been less violent. It would not have reduced the need for major changes in personnel, but they would have been made on a more rational basis, the atmosphere would have been calmer and the staff as a whole less bewildered and alarmed.

Language

Language is the principal embodiment of national culture – 'the Greeks had a word for it'. In other words, if there is a word for it, it is part of the national culture; if there is not, it most probably is not part of the national culture. Is it an accident that the English word 'sport' is universally used?

The importance of language in communications is therefore very great; it is an aid to penetrating the other culture and is important in understanding differences in culture and attitudes. There is no German word for 'fair' other than the English one. There is no Russian word for 'compromise' – does this denote a difference of attitude? Most probably it does. Without a thorough knowledge of another language there can be no real understanding, unless by great sensitivity and intuition, of another culture. Dr Max Gloor says:

> What is important is that the non-national market head adapts himself to the local scene, that he knows the local language, that he mixes well with the local people. You cannot run a food business unless you know what the simple man likes or dislikes and you cannot talk to him if you have to work through interpreters or if your social life is limited to the American Club and to the golf course.*

The language gives you therefore 'the feel of the situation' in a way which you cannot get through interpreters. But Dr Gloor knows that the command of the language will be in all but a few exceptional cases much less than perfect. It is in fact virtually impossible to know a foreign language perfectly, since it implies the adoption and assimilation of virtually the whole culture. The best speakers will make mistakes, and only under-

* Dr Max Gloor, op cit.

stand partially the more discreet overtones of what is said to them. If it comes to the need for 100 per cent accuracy, particularly in legal and similar matters, they will resort to interpreters if they are wise. Complex business transactions will probably be most safely conducted in one's own language, when the exact shade of meaning intended can be expressed and, hopefully, conveyed by the interpreter, who has only to translate the thought, not to create it – surely a logical and convenient division of labour? But Dr Gloor would still say that a knowledge of the language, imperfect though it be, is indispensable, for it means direct contact and there are many occasions, other than in love, when it is necessary.

There is another reason which Dr Gloor did not think it necessary to mention, but which is of great importance in the cultural context. Since a man's language is the embodiment of his culture, as we have said, and frequently the expression and symbol also of his nationality, the fact that the foreigner speaks it means that he respects its value – business, cultural or national – sufficiently to have learned it. The Portuguese is not flattered if he is addressed in Spanish, although he *may* understand it better than English. He does not regard Portuguese as a sub-culture of Spanish, so why should you have taken the trouble to learn Spanish and not Portuguese? The fact that you do not know anything of the other man's language is a statement that you do not regard it as important, and by extension that you do not regard his culture, and perhaps even his nationality, as important. In making such a statement you have obviously created a barrier which is one more to add to the number which must be painstakingly removed in the subsequent contacts.

The silent language

It is a commonplace that all nationalities use facial expressions and gestures either to show feelings or thoughts or to reinforce verbal utterances. The range of these modes of expression is much wider than is generally supposed and cultural anthropologists have analysed a whole range of actions which are part of the mode of expression in virtually all communities.

It is thus possible for someone to know the verbal language perfectly and yet fail to convey adequately to another nationality the full extent of his meaning through lack of knowledge of this 'silent' language. It is obviously more difficult to acquire because of its pervasive and subtle character and the fact that it is acquired unconsciously by the native; also, except for very elementary and obvious facts, it has not been analysed to a degree which permits effective teaching.

So there is little that can be done to improve skills in this type of communication without very long residence in the country concerned, but it is clearly important to realize that this is one more, perhaps quite serious, obstacle to complete communication across a different culture.

These, then, are the obstacles to communications – distance, culture, nationalism, semantics, environmental factors – of which account must be taken, whatever the nature or content of the communications, political, social or business. Let us look now at the business situation more specifically, that is to say, the content of international business communications, and the way communications are affected by, and affect, these other important characteristics which we have isolated earlier – increased risk and decision complexity.

The communications structure

In all discussions of international business management there is an undertone of frustrated concern that whatever the objective problems may be – financial, production, marketing and so on – the problem of communications may in the end be the most important factor in success or failure. The problem is, however, rarely faced as one problem since communications management is not yet a recognized discipline. The panacea normally employed is to introduce an interpreter, as in problems of language, but an interpreter perhaps of thought or custom. It is generally felt that if an individual from the domestic company can be sent to the foreign company he will deal with the major problems of communication, that is to say, the interpretation of head office policy to the local company, with any necessary adaptation, and conversely, he will know what it is important and relevant to transmit to head office. In many or most cases this only deals with the grosser aspects of the problem, and frequently only displaces the problem from head office to the local company, ie, the interpreter cannot interpret head office practice and policies to the local company effectively and equally cannot translate their point of view effectively into terms that head office will understand. We are not talking about problems of linguistics or even semantics, important as these are, but problems of attitudes and ideas, often never reduced to coherent statements, but underlying all actions on both sides.

As we have seen, it is not only the media and the means of communication which cause the difficulties, it is the whole range of factors from the actual subject matter itself to the cost of communicating. Not surprisingly, it is increasingly felt that this is a subject central to any discussion of international business management.

The subject matter

There is a plausible case for suggesting that the subject matter is the first aspect which requires consideration since if there were nothing to communicate there would be no problem of communications. It is in fact the *nature and amount* of information required at all stages which renders the subject so important.

First the *nature* of the information required: is this different from that which occurs in the domestic business *about* domestic business? We hope we have established by this discussion (a) that communications *are* organization and (b) that in international business the ordinary difficulties of communications are frequently greatly increased by a complex of physical and psychological factors. In this latter discussion we have been considering almost exclusively communications between the domestic company and the subsidiary company, or other form of local operation. This is by no means the whole story and a very important aspect of the matter is the internal communications on international matters both in the domestic or head office organization and the subsidiary company. We shall have something to say on the former subject, particularly when we come to the discussion of 'risk' and 'decision complexity' in subsequent chapters. Difficulties of internal communications contribute considerably to risk.

We have stressed the importance of communications in organization and as we shall not be discussing this subject at length in the present volume we think we should at least touch on some of the more important practical aspects here.

At the risk of appearing too abstract, let us trace through briefly the consequences that may flow from these difficulties of communication.

Physical communications

It may be contended that with frequent posts, and with telex, cable and telephone, together with rapid air communications, there are really no important difficulties remaining.

In the first place, of course, these are all *intermittent* means of communication, not continuous, as when people are physically in close proximity, even in a very large headquarters.

Secondly, all the verbal means require the ability to express ideas quite concisely and clearly. In practice this is a rare gift, and so there are frequent misunderstandings of fact and intention. They are also expensive, which tends to make the communications, other than post, shorter than is really desirable.

Thirdly, they are normally communications between individuals and not between groups, although the most advanced means do go some way to mitigating this disability. Discussions between groups are of quite a different character from discussions between individuals: a much more thorough exploration of issues can be made and a wider consensus of views obtained.

These problems are obviously greatly aggravated if three or more quasi-independent units of the same company are involved, as is becoming increasingly frequent. In the motor-car and other industries parts are now drawn from a number of different units and assembled in one plant, perhaps re-exporting the finished car. In such cases a very high degree of coordination about plans and deliveries between several units is essential.

How are these very real difficulties dealt with? Without going into details of different organizational systems, we can make several statements about *any* form of organization which is used to offset these disadvantages of operating at a distance.

First, coordination has to be recognized as a major requisite. Dr Gloor writes:

> Another main instrument of Head Office control, besides the budgeting procedure, is the personal contact. First there is the continuous writing and telephoning, but also meetings between the Regional Manager and the market head at least twice or three times a year, according to distance and other criteria. In addition to the contacts on a Regional Management/market head basis, there is a continuous flow of contacts on the secondary and third level which Regional Management tries desperately to control and coordinate somehow, but which have a general tendency to inflation.*

There must be coordination at both ends so that confusion does not arise through unregulated communications from a variety of sources.

Further, some intermediate coordination in the form of a regional headquarters may be necessary. Expressed in our terms of physical communications, these intermediate headquarters exist for two main purposes:

(a) to monitor the communications traffic;
(b) to select and 'boost' the communications of special importance.

* Dr Max Gloor, op cit.

Then the volume of communications traffic must be kept within certain bounds so that the network is not overburdened. The most important means of achieving this is by planning. Planning is a form of organization: in other words, it is anticipating what communications will be made in the future and thereby eliminating the need for them. Since planning occurs *before the event* there is more time for effective coordination and clearing up difficulties than when day-to-day matters are being dealt with. Here we come up against a serious objection, in that plans made with a certain lack of familiarity with the environment may be unsuitable when the time comes for execution; it is frequently said that one of the prime causes of the defeat of the French during the Peninsular War was that Napoleon instructed his generals from afar on what strategic moves they should make. Nevertheless, this is a difficulty to be surmounted, not a valid objection.

The policy of 'trusting the man on the spot' is perfectly valid as regards *tactics*; but the *strategy* should be a matter for detailed consultative planning well in advance.

The psychological problem

The human problems which we have explored briefly affect the organization problems from the second of the two aspects which we have noted when we stated that organization was (a) a system of communications and (b) a social system, designed to produce the most effective communications. The problems of producing an effective and cohesive *social system* from disparate elements, having different objectives and separated by the inefficiency of physical communications, are very great indeed, and yet without an effective *social system* the organization cannot by definition be effective. This is a problem felt intuitively by many managers rather than tackled in a planned, methodical way.

The purpose

Again, considered in our somewhat schematic terms:

All organizations, social or other, exist by definition for a *purpose.* The clearer and less ambiguous the purpose and the better it is communicated to the whole organization, the more effective the organization will be. In practice it will be evident from our previous discussion that there are great difficulties in producing a clear, unambiguous purpose, for differences of nationality, social customs, career possibilities, etc, all stand in the way. Nevertheless, the greatest effort should be concentrated on this factor, which is unquestionably the most important.

Social leadership
Secondly, qualities of *social leadership* become very important qualifications for managers, to a much greater degree than in more homogeneous conditions. An effective leader can go a long way towards mitigating the effects of ambiguous or contradictory objectives.

Communications in the social organization
Thirdly, the importance of *effective communications* in the *social* organization is very great, and more time, money and trouble must be expended on this subject, whether by international conferences of executives, visits of senior personnel, indoctrination in 'staff colleges', company public relations or whatever other means can be devised.

These are some of the more important implications of the communications problem which we have discussed. Their detailed working out, and expression in organizational structures, will be a matter for more extended treatment in the subsequent volume.

CHAPTER FIVE

Complexity

Business is obviously an extremely complex activity; this complexity is in some proportion to the number of factors involved and the length of time over which decisions have to be made. As business gets bigger the decisions get bigger and the time horizon lengthens.

There are still very large businesses operating essentially in one country but the management would not regard its task as other than extremely complex. It is after all a living organism striving to maintain itself in a changing environment – economic, social and political – and its cells, like those of the living body, are constantly dying and renewing themselves.

Is there then some special characteristic of international business which makes it inherently more complex than the same kind of business carried on in one country?

Most writers, whether academics or operators, recognize the pervasive nature of complexity in international operations. Here is a rather typical selection of references to it:

> Because the relative importance of external variables is so great in international business . . .*

and again, the same writer:

> Clearly it taxes the imagination to picture all of the combinations and permutations that could develop with respect to the human, physical and environmental requirements for international integration as they relate to the production and marketing dynamics of a truly multinational firm. Yet many more international managers of the future will probably be

* Salera, *Multinational Business* (Houghton Mifflin).

carrying out the very highly complicated integrating activities which now almost stagger the imagination.*

The Chairman of General Motors writes:

Unlike many of our other divisions, and reflecting the unusual character and diversity of problems, the Overseas Operations Division has extensive home office staff functions located in New York and Detroit.†

A study of the multi-national corporation has this:

However, these advantages can be more than offset by the greater degree of risk and complexity in managing such geographically dispersed operations. Instead of a single business environment influencing most of its activities, a multi-national company can have as many different environments as it has foreign subsidiaries.‡

Obviously all environmental factors complicate business and the fact that by definition an international business will be dealing with many more environments than a purely domestic one means that it will be more complex. Nationalism, climate, physical conditions, geography – all these and many more are factors which complicate the international businessman's life. Products which will fit one environment will not fit another, and so on. Later in this chapter we will have to look at the effects of these pressures and the lessons which are created by the response to them.

Before we do this, however, we will attempt a simple, perhaps naïve demonstration of the exponential nature of complexity in international business by considering one aspect of it. That is the man-made barrier to uniformity and free exchange, the one

* Salera, op cit.
† Frederic G. Donner, *The World-Wide Industrial Enterprise* (McGraw-Hill).
‡ Brooke and Remmers, op cit.

most specific to our subject, namely that of national sovereignty. Whatever barriers nature has erected in the way of international trade and finance, none perhaps is as effective as the enactments of sovereign governments. Without them at least the proliferation of subsidiary companies and the explosion in 'direct' investment would not have attained the massive volume of the sixties and seventies.

> Starting off with exports mainly from Switzerland and then from other manufacturing centres, such as England and Holland, Nestlé has been forced by protectionism, nationalism and other such 'isms' of the various governments to decentralize industrially so that today our goods are manufactured in more than 220 factories spread over 39 countries of the world including particularly Latin America and many of the developing countries in the Far East and Africa. Most of the markets in which we work have been transformed from original agency markets into markets in which our interests have taken the form of a local subsidiary company run by a 'market head'.*

Each country has its own institutions corresponding to the historical evolution, political and economic situation and governmental policies of the day. Even when the countries have marked resemblances in many important respects, such as the United States and Canada, or Norway and Sweden, there are nevertheless innumerable differences in the institutional framework within which the business has to operate. These differences obviously constitute so many different barriers between businesses operating in each of the countries.

Even in a comparatively minor matter such as the corporate form, whether limited liability or other, the fact that the requirements as regards directors, meetings, legal responsibilities, filing of returns and so on are different, means that each country has to be considered as a separate entity; a director of two companies in two different countries will not assume that

* Dr Max Gloor, 'Policies and Practices at Nestlé Alimentana S.A.'

he is fulfilling the same role in both, and through ignorance of the complex legal requirements may quite easily find himself in difficulties.

Each country has the right to make whatever regulations it sees fit, both as regards the activities of its own citizens, foreigners within its territories and the relationships between itself and each and every other state.

For example, in the case of finance in the United Kingdom:

● All the general laws on corporate finance apply to every company in the United Kingdom.

● Foreign-controlled companies are restricted in their borrowing powers.

● Companies domiciled in the sterling area are the subject of special regulation.

● There is detailed regulation of all corporate foreign exchange transactions.

● There are special regulations affecting the foreign exchange transactions of foreign-controlled companies.

From an internal point of view therefore a foreign-controlled company will have five different categories of financial legislation to comply with, of which only two will affect the domestic company. From an extreme point of view, ie, from the point of view of the HQ company, all five of these regulations will affect the relationship of the foreign subsidiary at some point. Moreover, these are five different kinds of regulation and their effect will be different according to the particular foreign country involved and the subject matter (taxation, labour, etc); broadly speaking they will apply to all the areas where government exercises control.

Whatever the subject matter, therefore, if the government concerned has thought fit to regulate it there are, potentially at least, five different sets of regulations to be considered:

- General internal regulations, applying to everyone in the territory.

- Special internal regulations applying to all foreigners, or foreign-controlled companies.

- Special internal regulations applying to special categories of foreigners or foreign-controlled companies.

- General external regulations, applying to all countries.

- Special external regulations applying to one or more particular foreign country.

Taking these five possible sets of variables together, it is clear that we have an exponential relationship varying with the number of countries concerned, and the number of possible variables is, we suggest:

$$v = x\,(2x + 1)$$
(v = number of variables; x = number of countries)

Admittedly this is only one aspect of the operations of a company, national or international, that is to say its relationship to governmental regulation, but here the demonstration of increased complexity due to the international dimension seems fairly conclusive. We do not think that there will be any other important aspect where international operations are less complex than national. They may be more attractive, more profitable, even more stable, but we do not think that they can be inherently less complex than purely national operations.*

A real-life situation might be where a business considers that

---

* cf, 'The size and diversity of these operations present us with major problems. We cannot confine ourselves to considering the relationship between two currencies. We are buying raw materials, selling exports, transferring dividends and so on in many currencies at the same time – and we have to think of all the relationships between them. We probably have at least twenty substantial cross positions to consider simultaneously.' Unilever Ltd. Annual Statement by the Chairman, May 8th, 1972.

it has two alternative strategies for growth: one to remain a purely national or domestic business, and the other to expand internationally. Let us suppose that these alternatives involve on the one hand creating new products and new markets at home, the domestic market for the existing products being saturated, and on the other selling the existing products, made domestically or locally, in new foreign markets.

Can there be a meaningful distinction in terms of complexity between one decision and the other? Not of difficulty, we must emphasize, but of complexity, that is to say in terms of the number of variables, and their interrelationship, of which account must be taken.

Of course, and no doubt because of the inherent complexity, in the case of the second alternative the businessman will find that he can get assistance from a wide range of specialized agencies – banks, government, export agents and others – and many of the difficulties will be taken off his shoulders. In the case of the first alternative he will be much more dependent on his own resources, but he will be operating in a familiar environment and the fundamental distinction may well be that in this case a much more creative activity will be involved.

There can be no question of a demonstration being possible in this case, but intuitively perhaps anyone who has dealt with such matters will feel that there is a difference in kind between the two cases. Why this may be will perhaps be made clearer in the latter part of this chapter.

Currency and taxation

Areas where direct intervention of government is most frequently encountered are currency and taxation. Changes in the relative values of currencies are one of the earliest and most specific new factors which have to be faced in virtually any international transaction. In the simpler cases, currency 'hedging' such as we discuss under 'Risk' will meet the requirements of the situation, but there are more complex cases where ongoing operating policies are involved, such as where to manufacture. In this case, the decision is to some extent based on relative costs as reflected in a given rate of exchange. Just how far-reaching the results of parity changes can be is shown by the following extract from *Fortune* published shortly after the realignment of the dollar:

The currency realignments of 1971, while welcomed for the stability they provide, have had some rather startling side-effects on multinational companies. The changes helped some competitors and products, and hurt others. In at least one case they dealt a massive blow to an entire industry ...

In some cases the currency changes benefited one competitor and hurt another because of differences in corporate strategies. G.M. produces its subcompact car, the Vega, in the U.S. to compete with imports. But Chrysler has no domestically manufactured subcompact; it imports Japanese Colts and British Crickets, which have become more costly since devaluation. 'There is a squeeze', says a Chrysler official. 'We have to eat the cost difference to remain competitive.'

The realignment is causing some consumer-goods manufacturers to change their product mix by making more high-priced items. Over the years, multinational companies have tended to produce inexpensive products in countries that have low labor rates, and expensive, technologically advanced articles in countries where the labor rates are higher. For example, Bulova manufactures a low-priced watch in Japan, medium-priced watches in Switzerland, and an expensive electronic watch in the U.S. When the value of the yen increased 17 per cent and the value of the Swiss franc 14 per cent, the spread in production costs among these products narrowed. Thus, the less expensive watches have lost some of their advantage, and Bulova is skewing its product mix toward the top of the line.

To increase their competitiveness in export markets, some companies are trying to shift production out of countries whose currencies have appreciated more than others. A U.S. drug company had been manufacturing proprietary drugs in Germany for shipment to the Italian market.

Because the German mark went up more than any other
European currency, the head of the company's European
subsidiary decided last Christmas Eve to switch this production to France. The move could be a gamble, however,
because the future of the various economies and their currencies is by no means certain. 'If I'm wrong', says the drug
executive, 'don't expect to find me in this job this time next
year.' *

The sort of company referred to in this quotation clearly has
widespread commercial relationships between its various operations and these afford an opportunity to take advantage of cost
differentials to reduce overall costs. This is not the only opportunity, however, and the possibilities of tax minimization have
attracted even more attention. By means of notional pricing of
goods exchanged between the various companies profits can be
made to occur, within the limits where tax treatment is most
favourable.

So far so good, but taxation is frequently an international as
well as a national matter, so the profits of a subsidiary company
have not only to be considered as bearing tax within its own
country, but those profits will frequently be subject to tax in
the country of the parent company. The situation that is most
favourable from the point of view of, say, three subsidiaries
trading amongst themselves may be the least favourable to the
group if, for example, there is no tax treaty between the
country chosen as the profit centre and the group company.
There will be other complications also, since profits will be
transferred in many cases as dividends declared by the subsidiary and paid to the parent. The dividend may however be
subject to special taxes, such as withholding tax, in some
countries and not in others.

There is also the attitude of the local tax authorities to
consider. Frequently they will have established some understanding of the normal economy of the local business and will
raise questions about untypical profits or losses and changes in

* 'The Difference the Dollar Makes', *Fortune*, February 1972, p 61.

the price of goods traded. So much so indeed that in our experience some companies have found it expedient to establish a fairly regular pattern of activity, even at the cost of some loss of overall tax advantage.

Since the activities of the multi-national companies have become a major subject of controversy, criticism of their activities has largely been concerned with their ability to avoid, if not evade, tax and to transfer funds from one country to another, whether or not it was in conformity with the policy of one or more of the governments concerned. There is no doubt that such activities have been carried on extensively, although whether the multi-national corporations are the main culprits is another story. Some writers, of whom the following is typical, have suggested that attempts at overall optimization would be self-defeating in very large companies because the complexities are too great to manage.

It is common practice among observers of multinational enterprises to talk about the use of (1) intercompany transfer pricing to avoid taxes, (2) the use of intercompany loans or extension of intercompany credit to avoid monetary restraints in the host country and (3) the engagement in currency speculation which weakens a nation's reserves. Such financial techniques have been used many times and, at times, they are used deliberately to circumvent national policy.

At least three distinct operating patterns have been identified among multinational enterprises. Of these, the medium-sized multinational enterprises have a greater tendency than the other enterprises to attempt an over-all systems optimization approach and more nearly approach the economists' concept of one 'economic man' running the enterprise from headquarters; even so, these enterprises fall far short of such a mark. Smaller firms, on the other hand, typically lack international experience and tend to have decentralized operations without close control from headquarters or coordination among subsidiaries.

The large multinational enterprises, which make up the third category, are more important economically than the other two groups and are the most feared by foreign countries. About one-third of all U.S. foreign direct investment is accounted for by a relatively few giants. There are at least three reasons why such large enterprises do not act as an organization run by one 'economic man' from headquarters. First, the organizations are too large and too complex. Obviously, a computer model would have to be used for such a purpose, but a model of a multinational enterprise with dozens, and in some cases hundreds, of subsidiaries operating in as many as 100 countries, with numerous interconnecting flows of goods and money, would be so complex as to be well beyond the capabilities of today's most advanced high-speed computer systems. As a result of this complexity, the managers use a variety of 'rules of thumb' to assist them in decision making. For example, they set equity equal to fixed assets in forming a new subsidiary. Yet, in one case a firm could have saved millions of dollars in U.S. taxes and still remained within the laws of the United States and the host country, had it used a greater portion of company funds in the form of debt instead of equity.*

This of course raises the whole question of optimization versus sub-optimization in the subsidiary companies, and we will return to this subject at the end of the chapter.

Those who have had a good deal of operating experience will perhaps be inclined to stress the difficulties created by fluctuating exchange rates and the complexities of international taxation, rather than the theoretical advantages of gain from currency speculation or the discontinuities of the international tax system, and this view is justified in the following chapters on 'Risk'. Certainly the problems of deciding what is profit from the point of view of the HQ company are extremely formidable,

* Robert B. Stobaugh, 'The Multinational Corporation: Measuring the Consequences', *Columbia Journal of World Business*, Vol VI, No 1, Jan/Feb 1971.

and there is no universal consensus on the criteria to be used.

Fluctuating exchange rates and differential rates of inflation as between one country and another are two of the commonest problems encountered in the consolidation of the accounts of a multinational corporation. Both these problems are obviously specific to international business. The first simply does not arise when business is conducted in one currency only, and the second only occurs to the extent that inflation affects the treatment of asset values (on which the determination of profit depends), whereas in international business there is a specific problem created by the *difference* in the rate of inflation in the HQ country, where the consolidation occurs, and the rate in the subsidiary company. This difference will of course also be reflected to some extent, and with a time lag, in the rates at which the one currency exchanges for the other.

In some cases the problem has been considered as insoluble, particularly where there has been difficulty in remitting dividends or where doubts have existed about the possibility of repatriating capital. The accounts of some multi-national companies have disclosed that the profits and assets of some subsidiaries have not been consolidated. A halfway house in the published accounts would be to report the subsidiary operations in the national currency, and some companies follow this practice.

Whatever is done, however, for reporting purposes in the published accounts, management still has to make judgements about the affairs of the subsidiary companies and needs some yardstick to use in the assessment. Some companies therefore attempt to translate the local accounts into terms of 'real' value, using indices of purchasing power. Even in countries of relative stability such as the UK there has been substantial erosion of real assets, at least over some periods of time, and profits computed in the conservative way have not taken account of this. Obviously in countries of very high inflation rates 'profits' may be quite insufficient to offset this erosion. The problem is further complicated by the fact that some countries, eg, Argentina, allow for at least partial adjustment of depreciation to compensate for the decline in purchasing power. The UK and many other countries with moderate but persistent inflation do not.

The pressures of the environment

What we have been discussing is in a sense the most simple or overt aspect of the matter, the pressures constituted by legislation or regulation (that is, by the State) on the corporate body, and with the effects of the relations between States on the relations between the parts of the organization. Here we are dealing with two rather definite entities, namely the State and the business, and the relationship can thus be observed easily and described to some extent in quantitative terms. It is the rather obvious core of complexity of international business.

When we come to the more intangible facts arising from differences in climate, geography, language, customs and the almost infinite number of conditions which distinguish even the most closely related environments from each other, then we enter a world where we have to deal more with effects than causes, like physicists watching the passage of particles in a cloud chamber.

We can perhaps look on the process by which a company extends its business to another country as one ideally like the multiplication of living cells by division. The business would seek to extend its operations without modification to include the new market in the same way as it would if, in an undifferentiated market, it needed to set up a branch operation. Whatever the purpose of this – sales, manufacturing, storage – it would reproduce the parent organization as far as it could, not only because of ingrained habit but even more because communication and control are that much easier between two similar bodies.

In a foreign environment, however, this process of reproduction is affected by a whole series of factors:

communications, as discussed in the last chapter;

man-made barriers to interchange, such as tariffs, quotas, visas, currency and so on;

the requirements of a new environment – sociological, economic and cultural.

All these forces will combine in a more or less unique way in each case to produce a new operation which represents the will of the parent company distorted sometimes beyond recognition; an operation which, quite frequently, may have neither the same name, ownership nor purpose as the parent.

The process will be continuous, the parent company in most cases conscious of the disadvantages of this situation, either real or potential, and striving to model the foreign operation to resemble itself, with the latter constantly seeking to adapt to the pressures of its immediate environment.

The tendency indeed is for the HQ company to seek uniformity everywhere, and there are two very fundamental and important reasons for this:

● The parent business is conscious that its specific expertise or superiority may be lost in the process of adaptation to another environment.

● The more changes are made at the periphery to conform to local needs, the more difficult the problem of control becomes; interchange is rendered more difficult and complexity increases.

The process is alluded to in the following quotation:

Multinational marketing lives in a world of paradoxes. International markets grow steadily more closely integrated as a result of progress and the expansion of international media. So tastes become more and more similar. Yet corporations dare not underestimate the sometimes subtle and sometimes fundamental differences which exist in different localities.

In any international management situation there will be a natural dialogue between the controlling forces at the central company, always yearning for simplification, and the foreign subsidiary which stresses the importance of local needs.

The central unit will often argue that people are the same everywhere. While this may be basically true, each market is modified by culture, climate and customs on the sociological side and by buying habits, distribution patterns and laws on the commercial side.

The corporations that have recognised the need for a balance between the extremes of a unified international image and adjustment to local conditions are the successful ones. Those who have not often fail dismally when they play their business matches away from home. . . .

So, if there is one lesson to be learnt, it is that international operations require high talent and flexible thinking. *It is a fatal mistake to ignore local conditions, but equally so to ignore the initial strengths which have built up the position in the home market.**

The writer here no doubt was not seeking to make a precise conceptual analysis of the problem; his theme was the more practical one expressed in his title 'The penalties of ignoring local needs', but nevertheless the use of the word 'simplification' is to be noted – 'simplification' is the antithesis of complexity resulting from divergent trends.

The reference also to 'the initial strengths' which have built up the position in the home market is significant.

When it comes to considering how a foreign market may be developed there will be certain preconceived ideas about the products to be sold, the financial commitments, the corporate form, local partners and so on. As a process of trial and error over a period of time, or after taking advice, it will be seen that certain modifications will have to be made to this concept. The

* C. Graeme Roe: 'The penalties of ignoring local needs', *The Times*, February 7th, 1972 (my italics).

market, local legislation or a selection of a large number of possible factors will have modified the concept.

> We cannot assume that what has worked in one place will work in another, unaltered. The price of success as a multi-national is endless readiness to adapt. We must recognise that the Irish like a different flavour in margarine from the English, that in the UK we can build up our own distribution of frozen food direct to the shop but in Germany we also use the existing wholesaler cold chain distribution, that in Switzerland fabrics may be washed in an automatic washing machine at 85°C which in Portugal will be washed in a bowl by hand at 40°C. Whenever confidence in our experience has led us to take the local conditions for granted, we have been very quickly taught that the price of ignorance is loss. In Spain, for instance, we did not appreciate the role of the barmen in the beer market, or the differences between the requirements of the small farmer in NW Spain for animal feed and those of the very much bigger farmer in England.
>
> For each country, for each segment of the market, we must formulate our package of knowledge afresh.*

If the company is contemplating a serious effort in the market it will be because it believes it has some advantage to offer over local suppliers. It may have demonstrated this by successfully exporting to the country over a period of time. Progressive involvement in the market may however require modifications to the product. It may be too dear, for example, and a cheaper model seems likely to open up a larger market. Or, if the company is contemplating local manufacture, compromises may have to be made on a larger number of issues from the corporate form, from the method of financing to the use of inferior plant or machinery.

In most cases the particular superiority of the company will however be a rather specific thing, and, as the quotation suggests,

* Unilever Ltd. Annual Statement by the Chairman, May 8th, 1972.

this may be lost sight of in the process of adaptation. Frequently the exact nature of this superiority is not easy to define, which makes the risk of losing it even greater. For a long period at least the Coca-Cola company would not contemplate the use of synthetic caffeine in their product, although it is known to be identical with natural. The formula had been so successful, and the reasons for the success so intangible, that no changes which were not essential would be contemplated.

If so much Scotch whisky is consumed in the world it is obviously because it is a good product sold at the right price and competently marketed. No doubt, in spite of some protestations to the contrary, the same product could be made in the US, just as Guinness is now brewed in London, not Dublin, but would Scotch whisky with the words 'Made in the United States' have the same appeal? Whatever advantages were gained in the way of cost, taxes or in other ways, might not something very fundamental have been sacrificed?

The case of General Motors' early incursions into the European market is very interesting. Mr Sloan, the then Chairman, regarded their engineering knowledge as the basis for expansion into the European markets, and this is confirmed by a subsequent Chairman, Frederic G. Donner:

> Two major considerations favored the acquisition of established manufacturing companies, rather than the construction of completely new facilities. First, General Motors was convinced that the most important contribution it could make overseas would be in the area of vehicle design and manufacture on a mass production basis. To compete effectively in the shortest possible time, the company would need a product with an accepted name and a strong marketing organization.*

On the face of it this is a curious statement. General Motors had overtaken Ford in America chiefly perhaps because of their

* Frederic G. Donner, *The World-Wide Industrial Enterprise; its Challenge and Promise* (McGraw-Hill Book Company).

recognition that the market wanted more variety, the Model T having supplied the basic motoring need. Management and marketing might have seemed the more obvious areas in which there was a marked superiority. Mr Sloan, in discussing his company's policy in England, Germany and France, emphasizes however the production aspect, being especially critical of Austin in England. The 'product' which he identified as exportable was therefore engineering know-how and not cars of a definite model, goodwill in brand names, marketing expertise or management.

Indeed, implicitly, he recognizes that some of these 'products' may not be exportable at all, and he states, for example, that there were considerable differences between him and his colleagues about their ability to tackle foreign markets *ab initio*.

> The one clear point of disagreement between myself and Mr Mooney concerned an aspect of what our policy should be in Germany. I viewed the case there something like this: If the idea was to make a very small car, much smaller than the Chevrolet – assuming that was an economical thing to do – then we might be better off dealing directly with Opel. I felt that we would get off to a better start that way than we would by trying to compete on our own in a country with which we were largely unfamiliar.*

It is to be noted that General Motors had already had for some years an assembly plant in Berlin, and a number of executives were in favour of expanding this facility rather than acquisition.

This is in effect the classic dilemma in international business; the attempt to reproduce the domestic business will frequently be a failure because it is unsuited to the foreign environment. Mr Sloan recognized this and with characteristic clarity of thought reduced the exportable product to a specialist engineering skill. By doing so, however, he exposed the fact that there were very large and essential areas of the product and the

* Alfred P. Sloan, Jr, *My Years with General Motors* (Pan).

company expertise where the company was deficient. The logical step is then to combine with or acquire another business having strengths in this area. By so doing, however, a highly differentiated activity will have been created, and indeed Vauxhall Motors in England, and Opel in Germany, are very different from General Motors US; Holden in Australia may be a little more similar.

To state only a few of the dissimilarities:

● Vauxhall and Opel, small – General Motors US, the largest manufacturing company in the world.

● General Motors US, the largest and twice the nearest competitor, Ford. In the UK Ford a market leader, General Motors with less strong position.

● In some foreign markets relatively restricted range – in the US a full range.

Companies all have a distinctive style, and the style of the largest and the market leader is normally very different from the others; dealers, for example, compete fiercely for GM distributorships in the US, while in the UK the position is likely to be different.

The position in Germany is different, with Opel (GM Germany) having a much stronger market position than Vauxhall in the UK. In Australia the position is again different; a relatively small manufacturing company having a very strong market share.

It is interesting to note that in France and Italy General Motors has virtually no position. Many years ago an attempt was made to buy Citroën, but was abandoned. General Motors did not feel it was strong enough to venture into the market using its own resources and as a result had done little business there until the Common Market made it possible to export from Germany.

W. R. Grace – European food operation

The case of W. R. Grace and Co establishing their food operation in Europe is interesting, as displaying a rather subtle and complex blend of factors making up the exportable 'product', as well as a very clear-sighted view of their weaknesses.

An overall policy decision had been taken to establish a consumer food operation in Europe by acquisition. The motives for this were essentially:

- the belief that the company should diversify its operations away from South America;

- awareness of the strength of the oil companies in the fertilizer business, already a field for diversification;

- a belief that the EEC would develop rapidly and afford opportunities for profitable growth.

The 'product' which could be exported to Europe was essentially:

- finance – the company disposed of substantial liquid resources;

- some limited knowledge of the food-manufacturing business, derived from various existing activities;

- extensive exposure to the problems of international business, including currency and taxation;

- a highly developed economic, commercial and financial research capability;

- very considerable expertise in the appraisal of businesses for purchase and the techniques of search and acquisition;

- a very sophisticated system of financial control through operating budgets.

It will be noted that this mixture was conspicuously short on management and marketing experience. What was sought almost instinctively, therefore, was a relatively simple business, in a traditional slow-moving industry with well-tried management amenable to American methods of control.

The concept of the 'product' was accurate and viable; it represented a sober analytical concept which required no more adaptation to the new market than is customary in the case of hardware or service industries. After about ten years the experience has been that important losses have not been sustained and a very substantial and profitable business has been created. This is all the more remarkable in view of the failure of companies with much more specific knowledge of the industry and much wider marketing expertise. It is well known that one of the largest chocolate companies in the world with extensive overseas experience failed with the acquisition of a German company.

This case is re-examined on pages 205-6, but it is worth while drawing attention here to the fact that W. R. Grace was sharply aware of its lack of knowledge of the proprietary food market, and of consumer marketing in general. Once a company had been acquired, the essential 'product' to be transferred became the financial and analytical skills of control and it was therefore impossible to compromise about these, whatever the local opposition.

The proprietary product

At the other end of the scale from these cases is the proprietary product, and the arch-type of this is Coca-Cola, already referred to in this discussion. Here the product is:

● the formula and the essence;

● the brand and its goodwill;

● the marketing 'package'.

Since this is regarded as the 'product', the ownership of the local facilities and the distribution is regarded as relatively unimportant, and the basic policy is to grant distributorships to local interests, provided that the 'product' is rigorously adhered to. Only the minimum concessions are made to local environmental conditions and the whole operation is mutually reinforcing on a world-wide scale.

In this Coca-Cola is exemplifying a general principle of considerable importance which might be stated as the *principle of minimum differentiation*; in other words, the complexity of the operation increases in proportion to the differences between the 'domestic' operation and the foreign operations, and therefore every business will or should seek to reduce those differences to the minimum.

Perhaps it was easier for what was virtually a one-product company to adopt a unified world-wide strategy than for a more diversified company. Nestlé, for example, manufactures a rather wide range of products and, while manufacturing methods have been highly standardized, marketing methods were largely left to the local 'market head' to determine.

> It is only since the setting up of a central Marketing Division at Head Office in 1961 that the Group is trying to teach itself that marketing situations and objectives for a given product are not necessarily different from one market to another. Though they may not be uniform the world over, they can nevertheless be reduced to a relatively small number and where the marketing situation and the marketing objectives are basically the same, there are not a hundred best solutions to the problem but probably only one or two. It therefore is to the benefit of all if this one or these two best solutions are worked out together and, subject to certain local adaptations, adopted uniformly in the respective markets.*

The same point, that is, the search for uniform company-wide solutions, is made in the following extract:

* Dr Max Gloor, op. cit.

The central headquarters concentrates its efforts on the basic problems. The spectrum is wide, from the quickest and most reliable way to monitor a test market to the most effective mode of management development, from the investigation of the emulsion structure of margarine and ice cream to the factors which influence the housewife's choices between proprietary and retailers' own brands; from the skills of buying in world markets to those of co-ordinated planning of the whole chain of raw material buying, production and distribution of the finished products. At the centre it is possible to put together the knowledge, experience and questions of the periphery, to deduce from them the universal problem, and to develop the line of inquiry most likely to lead to a solution of the widest possible applicability. That is why we do our product development in many countries, but concentrate our fundamental research in half a dozen.*

In formulating and packaging products and presenting them to the public it has generally been considered that the most important consideration should be to secure maximum acceptance in the market, but it is being increasingly realized that this conformity with the market increases the overall complexity of the operation, and there is consequently a point which represents the optimum degree of conformity for the operation as a whole. It is frequently very difficult to define where the optimum point is, but it is undoubtedly nearer to the domestic product than it is assumed to be. Of course, markets are also becoming less differentiated in many respects, but this is an additional consideration.

Product differentiation to conform to the local environment may be necessary, and indeed the only exportable product may be an abstraction, as in the case of General Motors, but such differentiation reduces the superiority of the 'domestic' company, exposes it to numerous additional hazards and creates

* Unilever Ltd. Statement of Chairman to the Annual General Meeting, May 8th, 1972.

barriers to integration between the different units of the group.
It is a primary source of additional complexity.

The human factor

This chapter is not intended to be a detailed examination of the
effects produced by the pressures of the environment, but
rather more a demonstration by example of a general principle. To trace these effects through all aspects of the business
would involve dealing with the whole subject of international
business from a functional standpoint – organization, marketing, production and so on – which is what we will attempt to do
in a further volume. Here we are concerned with the concept
itself, the concept of the parent organization reproducing itself;
of the changes produced in the offspring by its environment
and of the difficulties which this situation creates, as it might
in any family situation, in communication and understanding
between parent and offspring.

In every business there is a good deal of documentation, but
the essential business is contained in the minds of the people in
it. Anyone in industry has had experience of apparently simple
cases where processes capable of precise definition have failed
to work successfully without skilled personnel having an intimate practical knowledge of them. *A fortiori* the complex
living organism which is a business cannot be thought of in
isolation from the people in it.

In the simplest case, the domestic company will send its
export sales manager or representatives to advise and assist its
local agents, but as its relationships increase in complexity it
feels the need to send more personnel, so that its practices are
transferred as far as possible undiluted to the foreign country.
Those personnel, however, transplanted into a new environment are immediately subjected to multiple invisible and even
overt pressures and become something other than an extension
of the domestic business. Concessions of all kinds obviously
have to be made to the environment of the country and of the
business itself. They may be made smoothly, too smoothly in
some cases, but in others there will be conflict, as in the Dutch

example discussed in 'Communication' (*see* page 91).

From this process a new organism will emerge, with very close links in some departments, probably production and finance, and much more attenuated links in others. At one extreme there will be a perpetual and only partially successful attempt to make the new organism into a microcosm of the parent in every way; at the other, the new organization will yield to all the pressures and have little in common with its parent.

The effects of all these pressures on the chief executive, to take one example, are well described by Dr Gloor:

The third factor determining the type of man we need stems from the internationality of our company. About certain aspects I have already spoken, namely his adaptability to the local environment, his capacity of handling the local language, the problem of his nationality and I may add in this connection, his transferability which can put enormous stress and sacrifices on his personal life and on the education of his children in particular. But besides these personal qualifications, running a subsidiary of a foreign business needs particular administrative skills, as it demands certain personal restraints. I will explain the latter. Though running sometimes very considerable businesses, the subsidiary manager must accept that he has not the final responsibility to the ultimately beneficial owners of the business and many of the obligations of the normal top executive are being taken care of by Head Office, such as research, finance, etc. In a way he is a partly castrated top executive and it is as well he recognizes this, lest he remains permanently dissatisfied. Secondly, in addition to the loyalty to his country, he must develop a loyalty to the international company; the two may sometimes come in conflict, for instance in matters relating to transfer of profits at a time of stress on the balance of payments, or in questions such as whether a company should have local shareholders, or in export matters, considering the obvious tendency of the international company to draw its export requirements from the cheapest available source. It is granted that such conflicts can also occur within a national company, but allegiance to a foreign company certainly has a particular touch of its own.*

Optimization and sub-optimization

In the preceding chapter and in the two following chapters on 'Risk' we set out a very large number of factors complicating international business. The result of these and of adaptation to the environment such as we have discussed under product differentiation is that the foreign operations often have little in common with the domestic headquarters. They are then frequently relatively small operations in their respective foreign countries and suffer the disabilities of this position. The management may be semi-autonomous – 'trust the man on the spot' – and overall there may be a high degree of sub-optimization. By this we mean that the criterion of success will be results at the local operation level. Growth and profitability in each country individually may be satisfactory, looked at in isolation, but from the point of view of the operation as a whole, that is, of the domestic company, results may be much less than optimum. In particular, the areas where there is likely to be sub-optimization rather than overall optimization will be:

- taxation – there may be a failure to take advantage of the opportunity to transfer profits to low-tax areas;

- cash – cash balances may be held locally when they could be used to better advantage elsewhere;

- foreign-exchange exposure – there may be unnecessary exposure to foreign-exchange risk, or failure to take advantage of the possibility of moving funds;

- investment – there may be misallocation of funds through the failure to look at possibilities in other areas than the local one;

* Dr Max Gloor, 'Policies and Practices at Nestlé Alimentana S.A.'

- management – there may be a failure to move management to the most appropriate areas, in order to keep them available to the local company;

- integration of buying – each company may purchase for its own requirements, whereas global arrangements would be more advantageous.

Control

The centralization-decentralization dilemma occurs in international operations in a much more acute form than in most 'domestic' operations. As we have suggested, the pressures of the environment lead to increased differentiation and the pull towards local autonomy and sub-optimization is very strong.

Equally, with the improvement in the means of communication and the development of complex planning mechanisms as well as the growth of international trade, the forces tending towards integration and control from the centre are becoming stronger. The most centralized operation, given certain conditions, is, as we have suggested in 'Communication', the most efficient; and consequently the dominant trend, at least at the present time, is that of centralization.*

The process may be illustrated graphically as shown in the figure on the next page.

The area in which there is least dispute about the value of this is finance. The advantages from the point of view of interest rates, use of funds and risk exposure appear conclusive, and in any case the auditing requirements of the group impose a certain degree of uniformity.

A point is easily reached, however, where the fundamental operating facts of the business are obscured by the desire to extract the most from the integration process. For example, by means of notional charges such as management fees or royalties from one company to another, or discretionary pricing in inter-

* There is an excellent description of this essentially dialectical process in Brooke and Remmers, *The Strategy of Multinational Enterprise* (Longman).

company transactions, the true position becomes obscured. Profits are understated or overstated in a particular company according to the needs of the situation as seen by the finance department in the domestic company. Obviously these practices are accompanied by the maximum discretion in most cases since their object is to reduce taxation or avoid some local

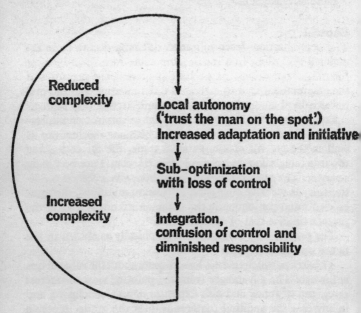

Reduced complexity

Local autonomy
('trust the man on the spot.')
Increased adaptation and initiative

Sub-optimization
with loss of control

Increased complexity

Integration,
confusion of control and
diminished responsibility

enactments. In consequence, many people are not aware within the company itself of the true position, and policies become distorted, incorrect assumptions are made about prices and profits, and management performance becomes difficult to assess. These are very important practical difficulties and militate strongly against the excessive use of integrating policies.

In some cases, but perhaps only with relatively small or tightly controlled family operations, there is dual accounting, but the risks and disadvantages of this preclude its use in many large organizations. Broadly speaking, therefore, there are only two alternative policies to follow, one being to restrict integration to those activities which do not concern management responsibility, and the other to create a stronger loyalty to the group than to the local entity.

It is this last course which is followed by the largest groups (perhaps the smaller ones have this loyalty anyway) such as IBM, Shell or Unilever. There is a continuous conscious effort to indoctrinate managers with a group loyalty and conformity to certain operating principles.

These are not new problems; the Foreign Service for many years has had to reconcile knowledge and acceptance of the local environment with loyalty to the home country. The practice of rotating officials amongst widely differing posts has been accepted as the best solution to the problem, at the cost frequently of familiarity with the problems of the local environment.

Many large corporations such as Unilever, Dunlop and Shell conscientiously practise a similar type of rotation and in addition maintain staff colleges where officials can be brought together at various stages in their career to be reindoctrinated.

Complexity has its problems, as Sam Goldwyn might have said, but it also has its rewards. The more exacting conditions of foreign business produce a type of executive who is more adaptable, less subject to irrational prejudice and more aware of his environment and its dangers, as well as its opportunities, than a man who has only had home service. In the modern international business the man with extensive foreign service may be the man of the moment.

The fact of this complexity may be viewed either as an advantage or as a disadvantage. There is certainly a considerable risk that a less than optimum solution will be found to a particular problem, but equally there are opportunities for reducing costs, minimizing taxation, overcoming trade barriers, and so on. Provided that the complexities can be handled (which requires great experience and expertise at the centre), then the multi-national corporation can have great advantages over an organization having less choice of alternatives.

A US company could, for example, take advantage of favourable tariffs to export parts from Canada to its factory in England, where low labour costs and favourable fiscal circumstances (investment grants and regional incentives) might favour more labour-intensive operations, and then export the resulting products to Commonwealth countries under favourable tariff conditions. This is a relatively simple case of a common optimization exercise.

The lesson for management in all this is perhaps that the centrifugal forces tending to create different policies in each country are very great and there is a danger of sub-optimization at the periphery. It is indeed very tempting for management at the centre to let subsidiary operations go their own way provided that the results are satisfactory. The result of this is likely to be a series of increasingly disparate operations evolving each according to its particular environment. In such a situation the organization as a whole may derive only disadvantages from its size and complexity.

The objections to centralization are on the other hand frequently very real. If the multi-national organization is to take advantage of its particular characteristics it must have clearly defined policies, particularly regarding product differentiation, and its organization must provide for:

- increased coordination, frequently through regional headquarters;

- management loyalty primarily to corporate and not to local aims;

- coordinating staffs of superior ability particularly in the areas of finance and marketing.

All this implies higher costs and the marginal profitability of each foreign operation has to be assessed in relation to these costs.

At this particular time, 1972, there may be a latent question as to the similarity between the conglomerate and the international or multi-national company. Certainly the conglomerate is complex, with many disparate businesses, and difficult choices to make as regards the allocation of corporate funds, or medium- and long-range planning. Indeed, the general consensus might be that the difficulties associated with the management of a conglomerate outweigh any industrial advantages it may have. It may well be that it is a phenomenon created by certain forces, political and economic, which have little to do with industrial efficiency.

Is the international business in the same category? We have seen that frequently the development of an international business is an unplanned, rather spontaneous, development on which only in the later phases is some policy grafted, when the commitment has become to a large extent irreversible. Certainly, there have been many costly experiments and not a few sensational failures.

But the fact that there is a strongly evolutionary trend in the process seems *prima facie* to place it in a different category from the conglomerate, which is frequently the result, on the one hand, of the opportunity offered when incompetent management makes companies easy targets for acquisition and, on the other, of temporary technical features of the stock market.

In the experience of the writer, at least, an international business created on the same time-scale as many conglomerates of the 1960s would have acute management problems and a risk of failure probably of the same order as the conglomerate. Each country involves substantially a separate business and strong policies at the centre are necessary if the whole thing is not to be unmanageable at the periphery.

In the last analysis there is a rather fundamental difference between most international businesses and most conglomerates: that the international business relies on a strong base of management and product expertise, without which it will normally limit its operations to least-risk formulae, such as licensing or joint ventures. The conglomerate in most cases appears to concentrate on the purchase of assets and earnings as things sufficient in themselves.

Many people who had observed Mr Jim Slater's operations in the sixties (in the UK) were inclined to wonder what would happen to the businesses acquired once the grosser errors of previous management had been corrected by the realization of surplus assets, economies in operation, and so on. Fortunately, he was as aware as anyone else that this was largely a 'once-for-all' operation, and having decided that he was 'not in the hard work business' the refurbished operations were floated off as independent entities, the function of the conglomerate then becoming that of an investment bank in relation to a client.

The nature of the process is thus rather different, although both give rise to highly complex situations. The position of the conglomerate appears to be complex without, in most cases, any compensating advantage; the position of the international company *may* become such that complexity outweighs advantages, but the art of its management is to ensure that it does not do so.

Further reading

Professor John Fayerweather, *International Business Management* (McGraw-Hill).

CHAPTER SIX

Risk (i)

'I'm a student of the downside risk' ...
J. D. SLATER

Surely, it will no doubt be said, risk is the very stuff of business itself, so why emphasize it as one of the more important distinguishing features of international business?

Certainly it is hard to conceive of business, in the capitalist world at least, without risk. Every day large corporations are seen to pass from apparent prosperity to near or total bankruptcy, and a world indeed where Rolls Royce Ltd, or other long-established and famous businesses, can become bankrupt, obviously does hold serious risks. The invention of the joint stock company itself, surely one of the landmarks in the history of business, was meant to deal with this very fact of risk. Capital was recognized to be of two sorts – that which was secured on tangible assets, where the risk was assumed to be minimal, and that which had no rights attaching to it other than participation in profits. The distinction between 'debt' and 'equity' or risk capital highlights this fundamental fact of most business activity. Risk then is undoubtedly a fact of most business activity in capitalist society.

An important technical distinction is made between 'risk' which implies measurable degrees of uncertainty and 'uncertainty' which implies the inability to forecast in quantified or even comparative terms what the probabilities are of a particular outcome. Management wishes therefore to turn conditions of 'uncertainty' into 'risk situations'. The use of techniques to estimate the probability of a certain range of possibilities, favourable or unfavourable, is very much on the increase and represents a valuable new addition to our means for turning relatively static estimates into more dynamic ones. The distinction between uncertainty and risk is an important one but in this discussion the term risk will also frequently include uncertainty; that is to say, basically risk situations where the outcome *cannot* be forecast within limits.

Risk, indeed, is not only a fact of business life but a fact of life itself, and far from declining in importance it may well be increasing. In the first place, business is a competitive activity and very large, easy profits are now the exception rather than the rule. The possession of capital may once have been almost a passport to profits and greater wealth but in the modern competitive world this is perhaps no longer so; indeed, while there is evidence of a cyclical movement, up and down, nevertheless the secular, long-term trend of profits seems to be downwards, and in established industries it has become difficult in some cases to raise capital because of the narrow profit margins. In these circumstances, risk and uncertainty become of special importance because the compensatory element of high profits for the lucky or successful may not be there. The calculations have therefore to be more accurate, and the risk of loss assessed in the knowledge that the possible profit may be modest.

There is of course an important corollary to this proposition, namely that it may be evident that the likelihood of large profits is remote and the risk very real, so that in the absence of some rational and quantified estimate of the risk many worthwhile things will never be attempted at all. We have emphasized the excitement and adventure in international operations, but this does not mean reckless plunging into the unknown; on the contrary, on page ix, referring to the author's experience with W. R. Grace & Co, we said: 'and the shrewd eye watching the downside risk . . .' This indeed seems to be a characteristic of the successful international or multi-national corporation – this ability to calculate carefully the risk in apparently unpromising situations:

It is understandable, therefore, that management frequently

appears to respond to this new challenge cautiously, and pursue what have been called risk-minimising policies.*

Again, one of the most successful *and* adventurous entrepreneurs of the post-war period is quoted in the following extract:

> 'We went for the easy overseas territories first,' says Slater. Easy means the English speaking countries, primarily Australia, South Africa, Canada, Hong Kong, and Singapore.
> 'I'm a student of the downside risk,' says Slater. 'My prime investment objective is to eliminate the downside risk and the risks seemed so much less in these areas than in Europe when we began to move overseas.'†

There is thus considerable unanimity about the importance of risk in international operations. We shall see indeed that the number and variety of risks is very great, but this fact alone might not perhaps justify risk as being identified as one of the major traits of international business. The fact is that there is a fundamental difference in the basic situation with which management has to deal, as fundamental indeed as the question of free will in Christian theology, the interpretation of which has split the Church into a number of apparently irreconcilable factions.

This difference stems from the fact that once the character of an individual business is determined the extent to which risk is accepted or not does not depend on management; it is a fact of the industry situation. There are thus high-risk and low-risk businesses; the extent to which they have this character is a function of the nature of the business itself, and the policies of management have only a marginal effect. Research intensive businesses are, for example, fundamentally high-risk busi-

* Michael Z. Brooke and H. Lee Remmers, *The Strategy of Multinational Enterprise* (Longman).
† John Davis, 'Slater's Next Ten Years', *Business Observer*, May 7th, 1972.

nesses, particularly where the development costs are very high, as in the aeronautical industry. Electricity generation and iron and steel are low-risk businesses; the demand for the product may fluctuate but there is little likelihood of vast installations becoming redundant in a very short space of time, as might occur in the aircraft industry. Management can reduce the impact of risk in the aerospace industry by diversification, by getting third parties to underwrite the financial situation, and indeed in a variety of ways which may make the difference between the success and failure of the enterprise as a whole. There are, however, only very limited possibilities for reducing the risks inherent in the nature of the industry.

In international business the assumption of risk is to a far greater extent voluntary; a business does not in most cases have to engage in business of a particular type in, say, Iceland or Bolivia – this is a policy decision of management. We have seen that in the initial phases of development internationally a business is likely to follow a policy of risk avoidance, ie, eschewing all risks, even those which might seem acceptable in the domestic market. Risk avoidance is, however, not compatible in most cases (it may be in some) with the extensive development of a foreign business and therefore, as we have shown in Chapter 2, voluntarily or involuntarily there is a progressively greater acceptance of the associated risks.

It is this dual situation of the range and importance of risk in international operations, and the acceptance of these risks as a matter of management policy, which distinguish the risk situation in the international environment from that in the domestic situation.

It might be objected that this emphasis on risk in the international aspect is because we look on the world from the comparative stability and security of the United States or Great Britain and not, say, from some troubled state of the Middle East, South East Asia or South America; this emphasis on risk may be a *question d'optique*, or of one's particular angle of vision. If this is so, then obviously our analysis is not valid; we are after all attempting to isolate the essential characteristics of international business, writing for all those who share at least something like the same economic system as ourselves. One does not have to go back in any case too far into economic history, even in these 'comparatively stable and secure' countries like the United States and Great Britain, to find that the operative word is very much 'comparatively' since, even if most of the world shared in the Depression of the thirties, not by any means everyone, including some of those 'insecure' countries of South America, shared in either of the two World Wars. It is as well to remember that stability and security are not absolute terms, and that a country like Mexico which seemed not long ago to be a hot-bed of violent revolution, hostile to the very principle of Western capitalism, now seems a more desirable place for investment than many others.

> Nobody can foresee which countries are going to be difficult. Chile was once thought to be a safe place to invest in. So was Libya. So, in its day, was Cuba.*

It is not easy to get accurate or meaningful statistics about losses which have arisen due to international operations. Once the emotional reaction is overcome to, for example, the notorious confiscations like those of the Bolshevik revolution, Communist China or some in Central or South America, the picture seems less clear. The losses of investments by, say, the United States, Great Britain or France since 1900 can be assessed fairly accurately, although in this particular period it would probably be predominantly investment in government bonds or utilities, not direct industrial investment. If it were the latter it might then be found that the 'losses' were not the original capital but retained profits, as some South American and Near Eastern governments tend awkwardly to argue. We shall see later that actual capital imported tends to be rather a small element in many situations.

Again, many of the losses with which we are concerned are trading and financial losses just as much as losses of capital;

* *The Economist*, November 6th–12th, 1971, p 17.

that is, the losses in ordinary commercial dealings and losses due, for example, to devaluation, inconvertibility, double taxation and the like.

The notion of 'loss' is therefore a very complex one, spanning an extraordinarily wide range of situations – at the one end very concerned with outright confiscation by a foreign, often revolutionary, government, and at the other with the losses sustained for example by Germany in two wars, as a result of confiscation by the victorious powers. We mention this fact because it still appears to condition investment policies in the Germany of the seventies, although it is not normally one that would occur in a discussion of risk.

We have thought it useful to introduce the distinction between 'risk' and 'uncertainty', and in this emotionally charged area the distinction becomes of some importance. The writer once engaged in a discussion on India with the then President of W. R. Grace, whose reaction was: 'a hell of a risky place'. It was not difficult to show that in fact investment there had been very satisfactory, and the comment then was: 'Well, I guess we've never lost much money in South America either' (an area where Grace have been important investors for more than a hundred years). 'Risk' here certainly meant 'uncertainty', ie, unpredictability.

At the particular point of time when we are writing (1971) Grace and many others have sustained very important losses in certain South American countries, but the comment on this situation in general is singularly revealing: the reasons given in the Directors' report for the divestment of South American interests is 'to eliminate fluctuating earnings'. In other words, it is not the profit position over the long haul, say ten years, which is in question, but the fluctuations in profits due mainly to inflation, currency devaluations, price fluctuations of primary materials (Grace was involved in sugar and paper production, for example), and sporadic political action.

Thus a fundamental factor influencing management against investment in areas of high *uncertainty* is the inability to plan. Modern large-scale business is very unwieldy and messages take a long time to travel either to the centre or from it. The result is that planning ahead, generally for periods of several years, is a necessity. Results of management on the spot are then compared with the plan, and the business is able to steer a reasonably steady course. If, however, the environment, economic or political, is subject to violent change, the plan is useless as a control mechanism and the performance of management has to be judged by other criteria than the achievement of the plan. In practice this means frequent and detailed examination of the whole operation of the business, to interpret the meaning of results, good or bad, to make provisions for unfavourable eventualities such as inflation or devaluation, and *particularly to assess the performance of management*. Protection also from the effects of unfavourable changes in the environment, or alternatively the exploitation of favourable changes, implies an ability to take quicker decisions than can be expected of large multi-national corporations. These are situations essentially suited to entrepreneurial management.

Frequently, therefore, when we are discussing 'risk' in relation to international business it is the inability to plan (implying a high degree of uncertainty) which is more important than the actual risk of loss of assets by, for example, direct confiscation.

Kinds of risk

So far we have been considering the subject in terms of emotional attitudes; the attitude that developed countries are less 'risky' than less developed ones; the attitude that arises from defeat in war – namely that any investment outside one's own country is risky; the attitude that equates risk with the inability to plan, not with the overall outcome over a period of time. So far, therefore, we have been concerned to say merely: 'Are you sure you mean "risk"?' But of course risk does exist and, as we have said, it is inherent in the very fact of business operations. Let us therefore look at the nature of risk and the kinds of risk to which the international business particularly is exposed.

In former times, the merchant himself would take his wares on long and perilous journeys, perhaps from Venice to Samarkand, and there he would exchange them for others which he hoped to sell on the way or in his native city on his return. He was evidently exposed to serious personal risks on these long journeys but these, although they are by no means absent in the modern world, are not as important as in those times. The merchant was also exposed to the risk of the loss of his merchandise through thieves and, perhaps more serious, losses through lack of demand and low prices either at his destination or when he returned to his native city. In most cases he would return with goods since money from China or India would not be convertible into his own currency on his return; gold, of course, or silver would be more convertible than local currencies.

The risks he was concerned with we would describe as ordinary *commercial risks*, distinguishing them from *currency risks* and *investment risks*, the three kinds of risk with which we are primarily concerned in this discussion.

The *kind* of commercial risk arising in international business is much the same as in domestic business, that is to say the suitability of the goods for the market, supply and demand, and price, but perhaps the subjective impression that this import/export trade is riskier than the home trade is justified.

But before we look at these specialized matters it may be useful to examine briefly what particular disabilities arise from the fact that the foreign company is foreign, whatever its formal legal constitution.

Xenophobia

The first and most obvious disability arises from the company's foreignness. The feelings which give rise to xenophobia are extremely deep-seated in most living creatures, not only man, and to a large extent the anti-attitudes of nations are due to these feelings, not rooted in any rational process. Many companies go to great lengths to conceal the fact that their products or companies are not native to the country and try not only to be 'good neighbours' but to take on as much local colour as possible.

> The acquisition would give General Motors the Opel dealer organisation, and we would acquire a 'German background' instead of having to operate as foreigners.*

Frequently, however, such a policy conflicts with marketing or prestige desiderata. In consequence the trademarks 'Esso', 'Shell' and 'Coca-Cola' are universally used.

The sense of property
The foreign company doing business is assumed to be there to make a profit, and it is supposed for a complex of reasons that this is in itself bad for the host country, since it represents something over and above the value of what he brings. He must therefore be removing wealth from the host country, and if indeed he is removing physical wealth in the form of minerals or other irreplaceable and natural resources, then he is obviously close to being a thief. 'The oil is ours' – this was a national slogan in Brazil and expressed the deep-seated sense of property felt by *all* men in *some* circumstances.

A sense of inferiority
If the foreigner is selling a product he is doing so in many cases because he has a superior product – that is his reason for being there. He will not readily enter a market already served with equal or superior products. The more the superiority is marked and the more essential the product is, the greater will be the resentment at this dependence on a foreign source. In the countries of Latin America this is a very potent feeling, and frequently drives them to set up competing industries even when there is no economic justification for them. A steel industry or an automobile industry is a symptom of national independence. Rich and powerful countries may feel the reverse emotion – if something is imported it is different and

* Alfred P. Sloan Jr, *My Years with General Motors* (Pan).

its possession may even be a prestige symbol. Until the United States fell into balance-of-payments troubles in the mid sixties, 'imported' was a prestige symbol. The knowledge that the nation was the richest and most powerful on earth was sufficient to offset any minor superiority. A small, unobtrusive country like Switzerland does not attract much resentment, however superior its products may be, and this widespread acknowledgement of technical quality, unaccompanied by any feeling of inferiority, is undoubtedly an important commercial asset.

The attitude to foreign products will frequently, however, be highly ambivalent; they will be admired and desired for their quality but detested as symbols of the foreigners' superiority.

Ideology

In any study of risk one cannot disregard political ideology. A marked swing to the left in a South American republic will frequently be accompanied by an antagonistic attitude to American business in any form, and a more welcoming attitude to Soviet, Chinese or East European business. Countries such as Indonesia have made radical changes in their attitudes to foreign companies according to internal political changes.

The effect of ideology will be partly a question of economic doctrine – pro or anti capitalism – and partly a political attitude concerned with countries exhibiting the particular brand of political *and* economic doctrine closest to that of the new party in power.

Businessmen cannot be expected to be sophisticated political analysts, and frequently make naïve assessments of the consequences for business of radical political change. This is a matter where caution and expert advice are required.

Economic importance

If the enterprise is very important to the economy of the host country it may well attract hostility on this account. If it is *not* important in the sense that it does not bring anything which is manifestly lacking, then it may attract hostility of a different kind, less virulent, no doubt, but less easy to combat. Countries which control imports or the establishment of foreign enterprises will probably take a much sterner view of the necessity for chewing-gum or cooking spices than they might of nuclear energy or aero-engines, if they have not the capability nationally to develop them.

Technical importance

Many countries will be anxious to acquire technology which they do not possess, and particularly continuing technology in areas where development is rapid. There will frequently be pressure for research and development facilities to be established in the host country so that local nationals will acquire at least some of the know-how. As long as there is a flow of necessary know-how the vulnerability of the foreign company will obviously be that much less, since the recipient will fear its cessation. The belief that foreign companies frequently prevent local nationals from having access to their know-how is an important source of friction.

Expatriate personnel

A foreign company that needs or prefers to employ non-national staff will obviously be more vulnerable in most countries since work permits will probably be required, and may be withheld if there is dissatisfaction. Conversely, the foreign company may wish to use foreign personnel in order not to lose its monopoly of know-how. This is frequently a deliberate and recurring problem.

The oil companies operating in many countries are required to teach the nationals to operate their wells and refineries, but clearly in doing so they lay themselves open to substitution at some convenient time. The Suez Canal Company believed that its control of the pilots was a considerable protection against expropriation, but in practice it was an illusion. However, in the case of the Anglo-Iranian Refineries at Abadan the possession of technical know-how afforded a high degree of protection.

Wealth

The greater wealth of the foreign company, if this is the case – its offices, the salaries it pays to its staff and the privileged position of its senior executives – all these are frequently sources of irritation and dislike.

Extra-Territoriality

Under this general heading we put all those factors which remove control from the national company to some other authority. It will be widely supposed, for example, that an important foreign-owned company follows policies which are intended to benefit the owners in the first place and the country of origin of the foreign company in the second place.

This is a subject of major importance which is discussed in a number of standard works dealing with the environmental aspect of foreign business.* We will return to it briefly in dealing with the multi-national company.

It may just be mentioned here, as a matter of considerable practical importance, that some countries have laid down more or less detailed codes of practice for the activities of foreign business. As yet, however, this is the exception rather than the rule.

Of course in most cases the effect of these attitudes and the extent to which they increase the risks to which the foreign corporation is subject is largely latent or potential. Xenophobia, for example, will probably not affect the normal trading operations of a company until there is some new and major factor in the situation, such as extreme tension between the country concerned and one or more foreign countries. In such cases the government may encourage the latent xenophobia of the people and use it as a pretext for discriminatory measures against the foreign company.

No doubt something can be done to erect defences against these attitudes, and certainly some of the major companies make quite an intensive public-relations effort in key areas. The scope

* See, for example, Maule and Litvak, *Foreign Investment: the Experience of Host Countries* (Praeger).

of any such measures is, however, limited and as far as there is any remedy it lies in the area of ownership and control.* This question of ownership is also of considerable importance in regard to other risks, since association with local interests may compensate for lack of knowledge of the operating environment which we consider to be the chief hazard, at least in the short term.

Commercial risks

In the first place the supplier is unlikely to know as much about the foreign market as he does about his own. He may be remote from it by a considerable distance and largely reliant on his agent or sales representative for information. He will not have the *feel of the market* to the same degree as of his own market, and the number of people in his organization familiar with the foreign market will probably be fewer than in the domestic market. He may be attempting to sell packaged cooking spices, for example, in Italy where the housewife is (or rather *was*) accustomed to buying fresh herbs or even growing her own. If the number of markets he is concerned with is large, his knowledge and feel for a particular market will be even less.

If we return to our simple example in the last chapter we see that it is not essentially the characteristics of the 'foreign' country which create the risk; it is (a) *lack of knowledge* and (b) *the inability to adapt to the new environment*. If indeed the example had been extended to a journey through several foreign countries we could have added a third characteristic contributing to the risk, namely (c) *the number of different situations which have to be dealt with*. The human mind has very definite limitations, and the larger the range of possibilities which have to be taken into account, the greater the possibility of error. The trio – communications, complexity and risk – form a nexus.

The situation will be complicated by the time factor; the

* See R. D. Robinson, *International Business Policy* (Holt, Rinehart and Winston).

goods will perhaps take some considerable time to reach the market, and if there are changes in requirements it may be some time, months perhaps, before the manufacturer becomes aware of the fact; in the meantime further shipments have gone on their way. The cost of transport may be quite an important item – it frequently is – and he now faces the necessity either of bringing the unsuitable goods back or selling them off at lower prices to offset their unsuitability.

It may be said that these things should not happen, that they are the result of bad market research, bad communications, and so on, and this may be true, but the fact is that they do happen frequently, and they are additional risks inherent in most international business situations. Listen to the Chairman of a world-famous company, BSA Ltd:

> You will notice that exceptional items gave rise to a nett charge against profits of £403,151. I told you last year that we had ended the 1967 season with stocks of finished motor cycles which were appreciably higher than we had anticipated. Most of these stocks were already in the USA, and we eventually came to the conclusion that it would be in the best long term interests of our motor cycle business to bring back some of these stocks to the UK and to give substantial discounts on the remainder. The charge of £729,200 arises from this action but is partly offset by a non-recurring profit arising out of devaluation.*

The second of our commercial risks, supply and demand, may be affected by a variety of considerations such as we have just mentioned, but again the risks will be greater because of distance and lack of knowledge.

Price, our third factor, will also affect supply and demand, and may itself be affected by a variety of elements not present in the domestic market, or at least not to the same degree. The three major special factors will be:

* The Birmingham Small Arms Company Ltd. Annual Report 1968.

changes in exchange rates
changes in import duties
changes in transport charges

and we must add to this *changes in the foreign market situation* in the sense that prices of the locally produced or imported products (from a third country) may have changed as a result of factors not affecting the exporter. For example, his competitors in the market or in other countries exporting to it may have experienced lower material or labour costs as a result of local circumstances. We have here four elements which are in a greater or less degree specific to international business.

Transport costs

Changes in transport costs are a serious source of risk. With heavy goods or raw materials particularly, transport costs frequently play a decisive role in determining which source is competitive. In the case of phosphate rock supplies to the UK, for example, freight costs from the cheapest source, Morocco, may be £1.30 per ton; from Florida they may be £2.50, at which level they will be competitive with Morocco. The rates are not entirely correlated but obviously a 25% rise in freights generally will mean an addition of say £0.32 in the case of Morocco and of £0.60 in the case of Florida, cancelling out the price advantage of Florida which made it competitive at the lower freight level. In the case of oil, the fluctuations in freight rates compel the oil companies to seek sources of oil widely spread so that they may switch supplies according to freight rates (and other factors). There is a wide range of commodities and manufactured goods which are sensitive to freight costs and where the competitive situation in a market can change very rapidly as a result of changes in rates bringing in or excluding different suppliers.

The risk in these cases is not simply a '*manque à gagner*', that is, the loss of *potential* business, but it may represent a real loss when supplies have been accumulated to ship to a market, and when there may be no readily available alternative market.

There may also be CIF contracts concluded on a basis of assumed freight rates, since the exporter is not always free to decide whether he will sell on an FOB or a CIF basis.

Where there is a factor of such importance, forecasting is extensively used, and since 'fixtures' are made some way ahead, in some cases months, indications of the state of the market can be obtained. Tramp freights, ie, largely non-specialized shipping, are particularly sensitive to large seasonal movements of certain commodities such as grain, and those concerned watch the situation of the grain-importing countries, such as India, China and even Eastern Europe, very closely indeed. Generally speaking, both exporter and importer will prefer some source of supply or a market not too sensitive to freight rates, however tempting the other conditions may be. In the phosphate rock situation discussed above there was at one time the possibility of supplies from Nauru, a small island to the north of Australia. The rock is of very high concentration and attractive technically, so in periods of low freights buyers in the UK studied the situation attentively and there were even some sales to Europe. The freight element was, however, about 500% of the Moroccan freight so that only small increases were needed to render it uncompetitive. The fact that Australia was the principal market meant that the sellers could get better prices from this market because it was not so freight sensitive, so there was a double hazard, increases in freights to Europe and increased sales to the nearer market at higher prices.

This sort of balance is frequently too fine in practice to make even low prices attractive enough for more than marginal supplies to move to the more remote markets.

In the case of the major oil companies the picture becomes even more complex because of the existence of many alternative sources of supply, the location of refineries, not always capable of handling all kinds of oil, and the enormous tonnages moved. Logistics constitute one of the major preoccupations of the oil companies, and in general they feel obliged to own substantial tonnages of tankers themselves, partly to ensure availability in times of stringency but also to even out the influence of market prices for freight, giving them an average freight cost which varies only within acceptable limits.

Import duties and government regulation

Import duties and other direct interventions, such as export taxes, imposed prices and quotas are more straightforward. On the whole trade between the developed countries of the West has tended to become freer, with less arbitrary interventions of governments. This does not necessarily apply to other countries which are not subscribers to GATT and which have acute balance-of-payments problems. While governmental actions of this kind are extremely disruptive they are rarely unanticipated, and an intelligent reading of the signs may give sufficient warning.

Import duties may seriously disrupt well-established trade and affect goodwill which may have been built up at great expense. This, therefore, is a major force impelling businessmen to set up manufacture in the country concerned, or at least to take counter-measures of some kind, such as licensing, joint ventures with local interests, or whatever seems the best way to avoid disruption of trade through the threat or reality of tariff increases.

> One set of reasons for deciding to locate in Canada was tersely listed as the 'duties involved in shipments to Canada, the possibility that the duties would be raised, and increased sales due to Canadian manufacture'.*

It is not always necessary to establish manufacture in the country itself; formerly it was rather common practice for US companies to export to the UK from Canada, thus benefiting from the preferential tariffs accorded to members of the Commonwealth. Mexico has become a preferred location for investment directed at other Latin American countries.

While local manufacture seems an obvious counter to the risk

* *U.S. Production Abroad and Balance of Payments* (National Industrial Conference Board, 1966).

or fact of protection of the market it has its own dangers, and there have been many disappointments. Indeed, in some cases where the market has been deliberately protected *in order* to attract local manufacture (the case of rayon in Australia is a classic example), there has been a marked reluctance to accept the benefits offered. Australia was an important market for rayon exports from the UK, almost entirely from Courtaulds Ltd, but the size of the market, cost of labour and materials, were considered to make local manufacture uneconomic. Eventually a plant was established but Courtaulds limited their own investment in it, and a large part of the capital was local. The venture has not been markedly successful. There is perhaps an echo of this venture in a statement by Mr Mathys of Courtaulds more recently:

> There are many reasons for operating overseas but preliminary considerations leading to the establishment of a factory overseas often turn on the feared loss of a profitable export market because of local production by a competitor or threats of prohibitive customs barriers or import licensing. Almost invariably the estimates show that to start with, and for some time to come, it would be cheaper and more profitable to manufacture in Britain and export than to manufacture in any overseas country. Almost invariably the estimates show that the size of the operation required to give a reasonable return is a good deal larger than that justified by the market surveys.*

In many cases, particularly in the less developed countries, the protection of the market is not the only inducement offered, but also tax holidays and capital grants.

The formulation of a policy in these circumstances has not been easy. If the foreign company has no stake in the market before tariffs are imposed or increased it will frequently not be tempted by the protection offered. If the products offered are

* *Planning and Managing an Overseas Business* (British Institute of Management).

sufficiently attractive they may sell well in spite of the tariff, and in any case it will be argued that the tariff protection can quite as easily be reduced as imposed. On the whole, in the post-war world this has been the trend, and some companies have therefore deliberately ignored the protective element of tariffs in making decisions about manufacture.* In the UK, for example, it was relatively common in the forties and fifties for manufacture of specialized chemicals to be established under the protection of Key Industries Duty, with a protective tariff of 30%. Some manufacturers, domestic and foreign, however, had a definite policy to ignore this tariff in making decisions about the feasibility of manufacture. In the light of subsequent experience, namely the abandonment of Key Industries Duties and the reduction of tariffs within the European Free Trade Area, this was a sound policy.

There are other features involved in decisions to set up local manufacture, such as the fact that manufacturing costs are low, as at present in Hong Kong, Taiwan and other Asiatic countries, or the desire to participate in the growth of an important market such as the EEC, or simply because the market cannot be served by imports because of logistical or other factors; but a discussion of these questions is outside our present concern, which is primarily risk.

The third-party situation
Before dealing with the first question we mentioned – first because it is the most complex – namely exchange rates, we will refer briefly to another potential source of risk to the exporter (and importer, who is also engaged in international business and must not be overlooked). This is the competition which may come in a given market from a third country. The example of the Birmingham Small Arms Company which we mentioned is interesting and typical.

Production of motor cycles in the United States had virtually ceased by the late sixties and BSA had built up a very substan-

* *U.S. Production Abroad and Balance of Payments* (National Industrial Conference Board, 1966).

tial export business of at least 250 million dollars per annum to this market. Export sales to all markets were as much as 75% of all sales, and exports to the USA were 80% of all exports, so its position was exceedingly vulnerable.

The chief competitor was Japan with lower wage rates, and a more favourable logistical position with regard to the principal market in the South-Western States. Wage rates were rising rapidly in the UK in the late sixties but so they were in Japan and it may be that the disparity was not being widened. The situation of the Japanese was *inherently* more favourable, however, because the home market was much larger, a market of 100 million people, to whom a motor cycle was still a means of propulsion. The export markets also were more widely spread. The United States therefore had not the same preponderant importance to the Japanese manufacturer as to BSA, and thus the position of the former was more stable; they could contemplate price reductions in any one market such as the US which would not affect too much their weighted average price situation. The market situation in the US was therefore extremely precarious for BSA, in spite of very considerable successes from time to time against strong competition.

The fact that marketing science has advanced to the stage where large campaigns can be quickly planned down to the minutest detail and launched without much tentative exploration means that risks from new sources of supply in apparently well-established markets have become a major factor in the seventies. The slow establishment of dealer and customer goodwill, and a long, slow process of fitting the product and the market approach to the local market once afforded a good deal of protection to the established product. That, in most cases, has disappeared and major competition may appear like Caesar – *veni*, *vidi*, *vici* – I came, I saw, I conquered. The arrival of the hordes of market researchers is now not long separated from the arrival of the conquering salesman.

Legal risks

Most transactions, whether trading or investment, involve an agreement of some sort. It may not always be in the form of a legal document; most frequently, indeed, it will be implied. When someone places an order for goods at a stated price he engages himself to pay, generally at a specific time.

The risks in international transactions flow, first, from the fact that the law may be different in the two countries concerned and, secondly, that the courts may be more or less impartial. In any case, conducting legal proceedings in a foreign country is complicated and expensive.

Generally the major risks are taken care of by stipulating which law will apply and who will be the arbitrator in case of difficulty, but risks remain and have to be assessed as part of the total risk situation.

Taxation

 ... the profits resulting from 97·5% of our turnover are basically and in many instances subject to double taxation and *there is the particular risk inherent in the transfer to the home country.**

In our rather naïve example in 'The Nature of International Business', Chapter 3, we pointed out that the traveller is greeted with suspicion not only by the authorities of the country he is going to but also by those of his own country when he returns. This is because he may have acquired some income or property abroad which is liable to taxation in his own country, and the authorities (in this case the Customs) realize that he may succumb to the temptation to say nothing about it, while their sources of information during his absence from the country are greatly reduced.

The complexities of international tax are enormous and all companies conducting business abroad are obliged to employ skilled tax lawyers to advise on the most favourable arrangements when two or more countries are involved.

The problem is largely that there are no common principles

* Dr Max Gloor, 'Policies and Practices at Nestlé Alimentana S.A.' (our italics).

of taxation, each country inventing its own system to suit its own purposes or ideology; there is no international tax law and no international tribunal to which disputes may be referred. At best there are bilateral tax treaties covering some of the grosser anomalies.

This state of affairs makes it possible not only to avoid paying tax to two countries, but to pay little or no tax to anyone. As we have mentioned, there are hospitable countries, mostly not of world-power status, which will offer a 'haven' to the hard-pressed international businessman.

We are not concerned here to discuss these complex and specialized matters, merely to point out that where there is so much uncertainty, so much complexity and so little international agreement there is, as Dr Gloor said, much risk of loss.

Financial risk

The risks we have so far discussed are of two sorts: those resulting from the remoteness, lack of knowledge and diversity of international operations – factors which are to some extent within the control of the business – and external factors, particularly government action. Import controls and other obstacles to the free movement of goods are important but on the whole their use has tended to decline progressively over the last quarter-century. For the pervasive reasons discussed earlier there has been an underlying conviction that trade should be freer and the ambition of autarchy or self-sufficiency has not seemed respectable or intelligent. Freer trade cannot benefit all, and so there have been and will be ebbs and flows in the tide, but the general trend has seemed clear. Monetary policy has been somewhat different. Convertibility was the post-war goal, the grand object, in a sense, of the Bretton Woods arrangements and the IMF. For a time it seemed that the goal would be achieved; the pound, the franc, the mark and other currencies became stronger and attempts at free convertibility, some wholly, some partially successful, were made.

But the dual objective, free trade and free convertibility, has proved too much. If the doors were open to the goods of the world, people rushed to buy them, consumer or capital goods, and currency crises were the result. The process itself is not simple, and the causes to some extent in dispute, but the fact was evident. Free trade and convertibility were only for the strongest, most disciplined and most competitive economies, and there were not enough of them.

Instability in the foreign-exchange markets has therefore not been the exclusive prerogative of 'unstable' countries in the less developed areas of the world. Indeed, while some countries such as Brazil, whose currency has not seemed the most stable in the world, were progressing to a better-managed state of affairs, the key Western countries and Japan have not always maintained parities compatible with the objective of freer trade. Some have had currencies which were seriously overvalued for long periods, resulting in progressively tighter restrictions on the movement of funds (Britain and France are conspicuous examples), and some have had currencies so undervalued that their goods have been far too cheap in their customers' markets.

Changes in the market values of currencies, which the national authorities were unable to control, have been the rule, culminating when the movements became too violent in upward or downward revaluation, generally compared with the dollar.

The world foreign-exchange market is a very large one, although the currencies of many major countries, such as Soviet Russia and China, are not traded in it. Nevertheless, the market is very large compared even with the economies of large countries. It exists to serve international trade and investment, and even those countries not participating in it have to use it for their international dealings. The Soviet Government is not anxious to pay in roubles and no one is anxious to receive them. A Russian or Chinese purchase of wheat or maize is paid for in dollars or pounds.

This market is a true market, although there is some rigging of the prices by national governments, and because it is a market there are speculative as well as utilitarian transactions.

Because there are speculative purchases and sales there are professional intermediaries, who will sell or buy currencies for settlement in the future – there is a 'future' market or 'forward' foreign-exchange market.

Two other basic classes of transaction are carried out by the forward exchange market: first, purchases or sales of currency which someone knows he is going to require or receive in the ordinary course of business, and when he wants to *eliminate* the speculative element in the transaction (that is, as soon as he has completed his transaction he wishes to know exactly how much he will have to pay, or how much he will receive, in his own *currency*). Then there are the protective movements of funds, perhaps by international or multi-national corporations. The *primary* aim in many or most cases is not to make money out of speculation, *but to avoid loss*. It is a motive like that of the buyer or seller of goods; he is concerned with the transaction itself, the economics of which he has calculated and which presumably are satisfactory to him. He therefore wishes to eliminate the currency factor, favourable or unfavourable, in the transaction; currency speculation is not his business.

It is obviously our duty to you as shareholders to protect ourselves against currency losses in this welter of transactions. But equally we believe we should not overstep the line between dealing and speculation. We should only enter the foreign exchange market in connection with ordinary trading transactions.

Speculation is not our business. It has nothing to do with making and selling foods or detergents or animal feeds. It is not how you, our shareholders, expect us to be spending our effort.

We like to do our business in conditions of currency stability. Whether currencies are fixed or floating, the smaller and the more predictable the fluctuations, the less worry it causes us. We do not like large changes accompanied by crises.*

* Unilever Ltd. Annual Statement by the Chairman, May 8th, 1972.

In many cases the international company, holding large liquid funds in a number of currencies, will take the same view. It does not wish to lose money through currency movements, but speculation is not its business, any more than when it buys an industrial site does it buy it with an eye to its future value on the market. If the value increases it will only revalue it at very long intervals, and even then not take the profit into the same account as trading operations.

There are therefore three classes of operation on the foreign-exchange markets: purchases and sales for trading purposes; speculative, by professional dealers; and 'protective movements' by substantial holders. There are grey areas, of course, round the latter transactions, for who can resist the possibility of profit when it appears virtually certain? When the devaluation of a major currency has become almost inevitable it is frequently not difficult to see *when* it is going to occur. The signs are well known and if owners of that currency seek not only to protect themselves against the loss of value but to make a profit too, then perhaps they are hardly as blameworthy as politicians would sometimes imply.

This is the background against which the international trader has to operate in what might be called normal conditions, that is to say, a market which does reflect to a large extent the realities of the situation, in spite of the intervention of governments from time to time to 'support' their currencies. According to his assessment and needs he can then choose from a variety of alternatives to protect his position, assisted by what are called 'professional risk-takers', that is, foreign-exchange dealers who, according to their expert assessment of risk, will relieve him of his risk by selling or buying his currency so that he knows at the time of concluding his purchase or sale exactly what the deal represents in terms of his own currency. This is a division of labour or of economic roles in society such as should delight the heart of any classical economist.

Unfortunately this is by no means the end of the story, because governments are apt to fear or mistrust the workings of a free market, especially when their affairs are not too well managed internally, or when their policies are incompatible with it, giving perhaps a desired result in one direction but creating distortions in their foreign-exchange situations. So there are a variety of forms of more direct government intervention in the market situation. They are frequently highly ingenious and since they are basically designed to defeat or avoid the working of the free market there may be no effective measure which the businessman can take; certainly the variety is too great for the market to have created in every case risk-bearing mechanisms, such as the forward exchange market, to take care of them.

These very manipulations sometimes create opportunities, however, and the 'blocked' funds arising from the refusal of governments to allow debts in their currencies to be converted through the foreign-exchange market can sometimes be used on very advantageous terms *within* the same country; so, films are made in Turkey and Spain, and investments are made which perhaps would not have seemed too attractive otherwise.

Exporting, even in the wealthiest countries, is a very desirable activity in the eyes of governments (except the export of currency and gold). So we find that most developed countries, at least, are anxious to fill gaps in the protection which is available to the exporter against those risks which he does not normally choose to run, chiefly monetary risks. One such is the credit risk, because the normal arrangements for international trade only cover relatively short-term transactions.

The banks will tell him that he can make a choice between CAD (cash against documents), irrevocable credit, or less watertight arrangements such as bills of exchange. Banks are not, however, in the long-term risk business, either at home or, still less, abroad; so when the transaction is for more than six months they may be prepared to provide money but they will not carry the risk. Special longer-term risk-bearing agencies, generally not providing the money but covering the risk, have come into being. One of the first was the Export Credit Guarantee Department, a UK Government agency. There are now institutions of this kind, private and governmental, in most exporting countries. Without them a great deal of trade, particularly with the countries of Eastern Europe which generally seek credit terms, would not have been possible. More recently cover has been extended to capital investment transactions in a number of countries. The United States has had such arrangements since about 1950, and other countries have followed suit, the UK being one of the later ones, extending its ECGD cover to investment only in 1971.

We are not attempting to describe the intricacies of an immense subject but to describe the risks to which the businessman is exposed and the degree to which he must deal with them, or more frequently opt out of them, if he is fortunate enough to find a 'professional risk-bearer' to take the burden off him.

Any international trader on a large scale will however find himself exposed to risks which he cannot hedge against, and then he has a problem which requires another form of technical expertise, namely, accounting. If his operations are on a large scale there will be purely fortuitous profits and losses, at certain periods perhaps quite large. In the quotation earlier from the Chairman of BSA there was a reference to a substantial foreign-exchange profit. The question how such profits or losses are to be treated in accounts is a matter of considerable difficulty. The accounts of an industrial or trading business are intended to reflect as far as possible the normal activities of the business and it would frequently be misleading to include profits or losses arising from purely fortuitous circumstances. Frequently, therefore, reserves are created in the same way as they are for bad debts; the reserves set up are sufficiently large to act as an effective 'cushion' against normal losses, and debits and credits are made to it according to the ebb and flow of good or bad fortune. This is a question of management policy which every company with its auditors or public accountants has to decide for itself.

Investment risks

So far, it will have been noted, we have been dealing mainly with trading and the risks inherent in buying or selling goods using foreign currencies. The subject generally receives less attention than investment but it has to be remembered, as we stressed in Chapter 2, that even trading frequently contains a hidden element of investment, representing the goodwill which has been built up by the expenditure of time, trouble and skill, if not money also, over a period. Moreover, in most cases 'direct' investment by manufacturing concerns leads to increased trading with the domestic company rather than less.

Investment, however, and particularly 'direct' investment – that is, investment made by corporations as part of their own businesses to create facilities which they themselves will own and operate – represents risk of another order. Hostages, in the form of tangible local assets, have been given, so to speak, to the other side. These are long-term risks with no professional risk-takers other than governments willing to back their judgement and put a price on the risk. Yet the volume of direct investment in the fifties and sixties was huge and was an appreciable factor in creating the instability in foreign exchanges discussed earlier.

A good deal of this investment was, it is true, in the developed countries themselves, US investment in the UK and the EEC, for example, and perhaps certain types of risk are less conspicuous in these countries; but there was much investment in the less developed countries also.

The reasons for the size of direct investment are complex. In the first place, much of this investment resulted from the very nature of the operations themselves. Oil and metals are to be found where nature has put them and, while there is a good deal of choice about where they are sought, only nature and luck decide where the deposits are eventually discovered by the geologists. Because of this situation and the size of the capital and length of time involved in exploitation, mining companies know more about the evaluation of risk than most people.

Secondly, much direct investment was involuntary and was made to protect existing business against loss due to import duties and transport costs, as we discussed earlier in this chapter. There are other direct motivations: a competitor on the world scene setting up in the country – Ford in Brazil, perhaps – which means that the rivals must follow or lose the market; a long-term view of the prospects, 'not a country of the present perhaps but, we believe, a country of the future probably'; then inducements of all kinds – cash grants, tax holidays and the rest. Low labour costs making it attractive to use the country as a base for export, as Hong Kong or Taiwan are used . . . the reasons are many and complex, as we have already seen.

The main risks to investment which have to be considered are:

- lack of knowledge of the business environment;
- discriminatory government action (see page 165);
- economic instability;
- unfavourable operating environment.

There are very few areas in the world where this order of factors does not apply. Even in the so-called high-risk areas the political risks are rarely as important as they appear and the stress we have laid at all stages in this work on the lack of knowledge of the environment would still remain. In the less developed countries, which are in many cases areas of greater political instability, the lack of information about the environment is frequently almost total, because of the poor statistical apparatus, and this may constitute a bigger hazard than political conditions.

Information
Knowledge of the business environment, whether in the domestic or foreign market, is always insufficient and every company strives to improve its information as far as is consistent with cost.

Estimates of the outcome of foreign direct investments usually involve a higher degree of uncertainty and risk than estimates relating to domestic investment. True, when managers make their estimates for a domestic investment, they are conscious of large areas of ignorance; and even where ample information is available they are aware that plausible estimates of outcome could easily cover a wide range. For foreign investments, however, the elements of uncertainty and risk are usually greatly magnified. As a result, any realistic board of directors places a heavy discount on the seemingly solid calculations generated by the staff. Instead of relying on such estimates alone, the international manager tends to undertake a foreign commitment by stages, making a limited commitment at each stage while learning more about what may lie ahead.*

In the foreign environment the need for a different frame of reference complicates the issue also.

● A major industrial company in the United States was considering entry into the European food market and commissioned a massive study of the market and the industry from a famous research agency. In the section of this study dealing with the British market there was no mention of the ready-baked cake market, worth approximately £100m. This omission was undoubtedly due to the fact that this market is small in the United States, other than for frozen cakes, and so the researcher had overlooked its importance, probably unique in the world.

● In the UK, conversely, there is the well-known story of the major US food company which expended large sums attempting to sell cake mixes, on the assumption that the UK market was basically the same as the US.

● Volkswagen, having decided on manufacture in the US, acquired a site and put out inquiries for various components, only to discover that no manufacturer would contemplate the

* Raymond Vernon, *Manager in the International Economy* (Prentice Hall).

small quantities required, quantities quite reasonable by European standards but insignificant by the standards of the huge US market.

Almost every company which has set up manufacturing operations in a foreign country would have its own story to tell of costly mistakes due to inadequate information, *in our view the chief hazard to be faced*. The check-list needed prior to the approval of any sizeable investment project in a foreign country would be of the same dimensions as this book, at least.

There is also the fact that the senior executives of the domestic company will normally have less knowledge of a foreign situation than they will of the domestic. Information about most business matters is a matter of daily exposure, and comes from an enormous variety of sources, not only specially prepared documents in the office. The number of people knowledgeable about a particular foreign country will tend to be less than those who know about the domestic market.

'POLITICAL' RISKS TO INVESTMENT

Discriminatory government action
In our simple story beginning Chapter 3, 'The Nature of International Business', we pointed out that the traveller appears to be discriminated against both in his own country, when he returns, and the country to which he goes; the fact of crossing a national frontier lays him open to many vexations. If the discrimination is of the kind reserved for the Christian in Muslim countries or for the United States citizen in South America, this is perhaps a small thing; what is much more important is the discrimination against his business activities, and this has become a subject in its own right.*

Expropriation
Expropriation is normally defined as compulsory purchase and exists in every country as the right of government. Normally it

* See, for example, Isaiah A. Litvak and Christopher J. Maule, op cit.

is only exercised for rather well-defined purposes such as the construction of facilities for public services – roads and airports. Domestically, there is frequently a right of appeal both as regards the expropriation itself and the compensation to be paid.

Expropriation, where it is not for the normal domestic reasons, from which foreign business interests are obviously not exempt, is generally the result of political ideology, or even emotional reactions of a xenophobic character. Again the list of important expropriations is not as long as might frequently be thought. A list of some of the more important ones is:

U.S. Direct Private Foreign Investment
   Bolivia, 1952, tin and petroleum
   Guatemala, 1953, land
   Argentina, 1958, utilities
   Brazil, 1959–60, utilities
   Indonesia, 1960–65, petroleum and rubber plantations
   Ceylon, 1962, petroleum distribution
   Iraq, 1965, bank facilities
   Algeria, 1966–67, insurance and detergent manufacture
   Chile, 1967, utilities.
British Direct Private Foreign Investment
   Burma, 1948, collectivization of agriculture, forestry, river
      transport and petroleum
   Ceylon, 1948, rubber plantations and tea estates
   Iran, 1951, petroleum
   India, 1955, banking
   Egypt, 1956–64, Suez Maritime Canal Company, banking,
      agriculture, commerce and manufacturing
   Burma, 1963, banking and commerce
   Tanzania, 1967, banking, manufacturing and trade

Source: J. F. Truitt, *Expropriation of Private Foreign Investment*, Indiana University, 1969 (unpublished dissertation).*

* Stefan H. Robock, 'Political Risk: Identification and Assessment', *Columbia Journal of World Business*, Vol VI, No 4, July/Aug 1971.

More recently there has been the sequestration of oil assets in Libya.

A great deal depends on the compensation. Generally this has been much less than the owners thought (or said) was adequate, but there has been no serious inquiry into its value. In some cases there has been a continuing relationship with the new national enterprise, as in the case of the Iranian oilfields, where a consortium of foreign companies, including the former owners, was set up to take over management and marketing.

Nationalization, which generally concerns a whole industry, affects domestic companies equally, and compensation is frequently in a form not particularly acceptable to the owners. Friendly governments also have not been guiltless of taking advantage of favourable circumstances to obtain control of foreign interests, as witness the forced sale of Courtaulds' US interests on the outbreak of war.

Expropriation in the world of today, where new nations are emerging and have strongly emotional nationalistic attitudes, is part of a larger problem. Generally speaking it is foreseeable as a likely contingency well in advance and perhaps, at the end of the day, it is not as important as common commercial risks in the life of a company. If the expropriator frequently acts from emotional motivations, the foreign owner also tends to be more than usually sensitive about this type of loss.

Harassment

It may well be that the placing of obstacles in the way of the foreign company is a much more widespread and more important type of risk. The British operator in the Far East has had to accustom himself for at least a century to what became known as 'the squeeze'. The Chinese were considered to be adept at finding ingenious ways to make the foreigner pay for the privilege of doing business. From the point of view of the foreign businessman this form of risk is probably the worst because it is generally gradual, intermittent, being relaxed when the circumstances are unfavourable, and difficult to forecast in so far as the outcome is concerned. There is always the possibility that the profitability of the enterprise may be so reduced that there is no other course of action but sale under confiscatory terms to the host country. This is a situation in which many public utilities have found themselves in the period when it was common for trams, railways and other public utilities to be foreign-owned in Russia and South America. Restriction on raising rates was a commonly used method to force the sale of the facilities to local interests, public or private. In the case of natural-resource companies, royalties, excise taxes, labour regulations and rates of extraction are some of the commonly used expedients to obtain more revenue or force a sale by harassment.

This form of 'squeeze' may be more effective when a number of host countries combine as they have done in OPEC, the Organization of Petroleum Exporting Countries, to obtain better terms from the international oil companies.

This type of risk applies to developed and supposedly liberal countries as well as others. The British Government has exerted much pressure on foreign-owned drug companies to reduce prices of 'essential' drugs in the UK and the methods used have not been greatly different from those which British multi-national companies would deplore if used against them in a foreign country: suspension of patent rights and encouragement of doubtful foreign producers to flout international standards of patent observance. The '*sacro egoismo*' of the State proclaimed by Mussolini is never far away in dealings with another country. The 'squeeze' then is one of the most pervasive, most important and least studied aspects of international business.

Unfavourable operating environment

In 1971 Henry Ford II paid a visit to the UK and disclosed that his company would not proceed with certain investment plans because of unfavourable labour attitudes. From the point of view of stability and security for foreign investment the UK has probably a better record than most countries, but this is not always enough to offset other factors. The attitude of the labour unions in France undoubtedly compounded the difficulties of General Electric with Machines Bull. Other examples in developed countries could be found quite easily.

In some less developed countries there are problems of rather a different order: the use of 'strong-arm' methods to defend local monopolies; assassination or intimidation of personnel; persistent pressure by the authorities of an extra-legal kind . . . there is a long list of such tactics. Official approval for establishment in *any* foreign country is not sufficient to ensure the same conditions as govern the operations of domestic companies.

Economic instability

Economic instability is generally thought of as a concomitant of political instability. It frequently is, particularly in the less developed countries, but it is certainly not confined to them. The situation in many highly respectable countries, politically at least, has needed constant vigilance. France, the UK, the United States . . . these are not generally thought of as politically unstable countries, and yet they have by no means been free of economic problems in the sixties and seventies.

Economic instability may take a number of different forms of concern to the foreign investor:

rapid inflation;

changes of interest rates within wide margins, making the cost of borrowed funds unpredictable;

shortage of capital, for fixed or working capital purposes;

changes in exchange rates;

restriction on the remittance of profits and dividends;

restriction on local borrowing;

changes in tax structure.

These are all relatively technical matters, each requiring detailed and expert knowledge. It is necessary to say here, however, that each of these matters needs careful consideration in the case of investment in *any* country, not merely in those which have a bad record in the past. They are to some extent at least contagious and may be the result of external circumstances. The late sixties and seventies have seen some retreat from free convertibility and an international code of behaviour, and it may well be that more restrictions for a time at least will be the order of the day. The formation of trading blocs such as the EEC may ensure relative stability in quite large areas, but the relationship between the blocs may be characterized by instability as regards a number of the matters mentioned.

Political instability

It is not unintentional that we list this aspect last. It features, as we said earlier, too prominently in most discussions of risk in international business, and in any case is less easy to forecast than most of the other elements of risk which we have discussed. Within the last quarter-century there have been marked changes in the political status of many countries. These things are at worst relative and the prospect of violent revolution and confiscation is only one of the factors to be assessed in a complex picture.

Moreover, just as commercial risks may be hedged, at a price, with professional risk-takers, some at least of the risks in some unstable areas may be hedged with government or international agencies. Most developed countries have private or government credit assurance; counterpart funds are available to put alongside private capital and frequently special deals may be concluded direct with governments if the project concerned is considered sufficiently important in the national interest of the country in question. In any consideration of an otherwise attractive proposition, political risk is best left as the last factor for appraisal, and in many cases if the proposition is attractive in other respects means can be found to deal with the so-called political risk.

Summary

In the first part of the study of risk as a major feature of international business, we have been concerned to distinguish between uncertainty, which is the inability to quantify or define the risk situation, and risk proper. It is from the former that the business organization recoils. We have discussed briefly the wide array of risks, particularly commercial, currency and investment risks. It is the lack of knowledge of the market and the environment, not political risk (or more usually uncertainty), which is the major factor. We now pass to a consideration of different risk policies. Involvement in foreign business requires a risk policy when domestic business may not, because whereas in the domestic situation it is imposed, ie, it is a fact of the environment, in foreign business it represents a choice.

CHAPTER SEVEN

Risk (ii)

In the last chapter we have listed and discussed to some extent a formidable number of risks. It is not surprising that experience or knowledge of even a few of these is sufficient to deter many organizations from any major international effort. Anyone who has ever attempted to get acceptance for a project in a new area overseas, or of a new type, knows how many arguments are raised against it, almost all related to risks of various kinds. The fact that the risks mentioned are often the wrong ones does not make the process easier. It is therefore to be expected that the major part of the principal countries' overseas business will be in the hands of a small number of companies, reported to be about 600 in the United States and 100 in the United Kingdom. It is not so much perhaps a question of having the products or indeed the resources to exploit the market, but rather the familiarity with the environment of foreign business so that the risks are seen in perspective and can be dealt with systematically.

Obviously, with so much fear, if not knowledge, of the risks involved each company will have some kind of risk policy. There will have been discussions at managerial or board level from time to time, if only about propositions for development abroad which have been brought by agents or other outside parties. Such discussions over a period of time will have crystallized into a general doctrine about the extent to which the company is interested in international business, and what are regarded as reasonable risks. In most cases this doctrine will be implicit; that is, it will be perhaps more of a corporate attitude than a logical policy, whereas the major international companies will have explicit policies, that is, policies formulated, discussed and adopted as part of the overall policy structure of the business. The more the implicit type of policy is analysed and rendered explicit, the more likely it is to be realistic and satisfactory, rather than impressionistic.

In discussing the motivation of the businessman in engaging in foreign business, we examined in Chapter 1 a large number of factors which play a role in this respect, while in the description of the 'Phases in the Development of an International Business' (Chapter 2) we touched on the question of risk policies. In the earliest phase, which we called opportunistic, there is no conscious commitment at all to foreign business, and the major objective of the businessman is to obtain some adventitious profit with minimum involvement and *no risk*. We said there: 'His decision may probably be to treat export as a marginal factor in his production plan, useful for absorbing spare capacity and spreading expenses, but otherwise too risky or in other respects undesirable', and we summarized his position as follows: '*In this first phase all or the great majority of the options taken will have been those which involve least risk and disturbance to his ordinary business; he will refuse definite commitment of any magnitude or for any long period of time. The approach is essentially opportunistic.*'

Phase II we described as being of 'limited commitment', involving some voluntary involvement in seeking further business, provided that it can be satisfied with the use of marginal production capacity. At this stage the exporter will not consciously have modified his attitude to risk, but he will in fact have created a capital asset in the foreign market, in the form of goodwill, and to this extent he will have accepted an additional element of risk. If he now withdraws he will lose the benefit of his development of the market.

Phase III we have described as the phase of 'limited fixed investment' (in the home country principally), when the policy of using only marginal capacity has been abandoned. 'The characteristic of this phase is thus a voluntary and extensive commitment to foreign business, still regarded, however, as ancillary to the domestic business, to an extent which would prevent failure of the foreign business from seriously affecting the performance of the business as a whole.'

There is therefore in this phase an acceptance of risk in a variety of forms, whether as regards exports, the installation of incremental manufacturing capacity to supply them, or even limited investment in foreign countries. The overriding risk policy is, however, based on a limitation of the foreign business to an extent which would not seriously affect the overall trading and financial position of the domestic company. Such is obviously the policy of most small and even medium-sized businesses in the UK at the present, as well as in the United States.

This is not invariably the case, however, and there are a number of medium-sized businesses in the UK which have allowed themselves to become heavily dependent on the US market particularly. At the time this study is being written BSA, which has already been mentioned, is in serious difficulties; Lines Bros and Lesney Products, successful toy manufacturers, have also become the victims of their own success in the US market. These companies had obviously no explicit risk policy: recently, indeed, the new management of BSA Ltd has stated that steps were being taken to reduce the dependence on the US market, implying that the previous policy had not correctly assessed the risk.

We describe our Phase IV as 'major dependence on foreign business'. The companies just mentioned had obviously entered this phase, and even passed beyond it to the stage when the business is almost entirely dependent on foreign business. The fact is, however, that if the company does become so dependent it has to evolve a risk policy to deal with this situation, and not conduct its business as if it were still in Phase III, 'limited dependence on foreign business'.

Development of a sophisticated risk policy

Clearly, as long as the overall policy is to limit involvement in foreign business so that it cannot affect unfavourably, to any material extent, the assets or earnings of the business, this normally constitutes the main feature of the risk policy. The treatment of risk on a day-to-day basis will not involve any very sophisticated policy discussions. The normal pattern will be somewhat as follows:

- The major part of foreign sales will be as exports, with a spread of markets normally restricted to those regarded as reasonably safe.

- In other markets, credit insurance will be taken out and involvement treated as a short-term exercise.

- Credit terms, the placing of consignment stocks, and so on, will be handled on a 'risk minimizing' basis.

- Foreign exchange will be bought or sold forward in virtually all cases to cover this risk.

- Any investment in subsidiary companies will be restricted basically to those countries regarded as sound, such as (in the case of the US) the UK and Canada; (in the case of the UK) Australia, perhaps Holland (but not the US because of its size and competitive strength).

- Beyond a relatively small initial investment expansion will be financed from profits.

A policy of which these are the principal characteristics is not concerned with maximizing profits, nor will there be any serious attempt to assess the risk inherent in any particular situation. The policy will be one of empirical risk minimization.

It is only in fact in Phase IV – 'major dependence on foreign business' – that the need for a definite risk policy of a more positive than negative kind is felt. It is quite true that even very large international companies are extremely cautious and frequently, as Messrs Brooke and Remmers say, they follow 'risk minimizing policies', but this is a different thing from 'risk avoidance', which is essentially the policy with most companies in the earlier phases of development. Indeed, 'risk minimizing' is almost the concomitant of following a more positive policy;

no company will voluntarily expose itself to more risk than necessary in carrying out its chosen trading or financial policies, but this is quite a different thing from deciding, as a matter of policy, to avoid risk, and *in this context we mean risk not in any absolute sense but any risk greater than is normally encountered in the domestic operations.*

In this phase we have said that 'the overall performance of the company is heavily but not overwhelmingly dependent on foreign business'. By definition, therefore, the business will be exposed to special risks in a variety of ways and management will have developed a good deal of sophistication in dealing with the more technical aspects, particularly of financial risk, although it may still be some way from developing any kind of really coherent overall risk policy. In other words, it will have outgrown the phases of 'risk avoidance' but it may not yet feel itself sufficiently vulnerable to have developed specific risk policies. This is therefore rather a dangerous phase in the life of a business and cases of serious difficulties are fairly common. In the next and final phase, that of the multi-national corporation, there can be no question of *not* having a risk policy.

Even this last statement may require some justification. Should not even the largest companies avoid risk, as we have seen that smaller companies try to do? There are many reasons why in general they do not and, indeed, cannot.

- The variety of risks is so great and the time and place of their occurrence so unforeseeable that risk avoidance would condemn anyone following such a policy to exclusion from virtually all foreign markets at some time.

- If there are risks there will be less competition, for reasons which must now be obvious; indeed, the world may be divided in a sense into 'safe' markets, where competition is intense, and 'unsafe' markets where competition is virtually non-existent.

- Markets which are unsafe to some operators are safer to others; as we have said, 'one man's uncertainty is another man's risk'. There is always risk (or uncertainty) but the experienced operator can frequently turn an 'uncertainty' situation into a 'risk' situation.

● The large company may have a tax situation enabling it to offset losses in one market against profits in another.

● The large company will have a wide spread of risks of various kinds.

Of course, the attitude of even the largest industrial corporation is very different from that of the professional risk-bearer, who makes his profit out of the accurate assessment of risk and a complex, specialized array of techniques for dealing with it. *Their attitude has been described as 'risk minimizing',* that is, they accept the necessity for incurring risk but, since risk bearing is not their business, seek to reduce it wherever possible.*†

There are therefore in practice three kinds of policy:

　　risk-avoidance;
　　risk-minimizing;
　　risk-bearing;

and our discussion is obviously concerned chiefly with the second category, that is to say, with those who, for adequate compensatory advantage, are prepared to incur certain risks but will seek to minimize their probability or impact, and will not normally play the role of professional risk-taker in, for example, such matters as currency speculation. Their policies are likely to be defensive, to protect their commercial profits, rather than offensive, that is, to increase them by gains arising from the assessment of non-commercial risk.

* By Brooke and Remmers.
† In the NICB study only one corporation said that its policy was to avoid risk (*U.S. Production Abroad and Balance of Payments*, National Industrial Conference Board, 1966).

The nature and objectives of a risk-minimizing policy

We have thus recognized a fundamental distinction between risk-avoidance and risk-minimizing policies. In Chapter 2 we showed how, almost imperceptibly, a company which has based its policy on *risk avoidance* slips into a situation where it has created a capital asset, namely a market position, in the foreign country. *It is the creation of this asset which leads to the transition from risk avoidance to risk minimization in the majority of cases.* The company now wishes to protect its position and its attitude shifts to the minimum risk policy which will accomplish this.

Organizations which are not concerned with markets to the same extent, such as natural-resources companies, have, as we stressed earlier, a different order of motivation; in effect they have to go where their discoveries lead them and then follow whatever risk-minimizing policies appear to be appropriate.

In considering a risk-minimizing policy each company will have problems peculiar to itself, and will have to consider the causes of its vulnerability and the measures which it can take for its protection.

Vulnerability to risk

A useful approach to the formulation of a risk policy is to set out the situation of the company in terms of the chief risks likely to be encountered. This may well indicate the action to be taken to reduce vulnerability.

We have taken the principal factors in a business which are subject to outside influence and have made a rough and perhaps controversial assessment of them under three headings, namely, political action, commercial risks and financial risks (Table A). To illustrate this simple piece of methodology let us take 1. Land. Under the heading 'Political action' we have put 'High', indicating not that there is anything about the nature of land which makes it particularly vulnerable to political action but that *if* political action is taken against the business there is no way in which land can be protected from confiscation or nationalization. We have put 'Low' under both the 'Commercial' and 'Financial' risks because there is not normally any great vulnerability to land in commercial situations, while the risks to land values arising, for example, from devaluation or other financial developments are generally negligible; land is a better 'store of value' than money. The exception to this may be land whose principal value is in mineral deposits.

TABLE A

VULNERABILITY TO VARIOUS FORMS OF RISK

	Political action	Commercial risks	Financial risks
1. Land	High	Low	Low
2. Buildings	High	Average	Low
3. Manufacturing equipment	High	Average	Low
4. Transport equipment	Average	Average	Low
5. Raw materials	High	Average	High
6. Working capital	High	Average	High
7. Skilled staff	Average	Average	Average
8. Labour	Average/ high	Average	High
9. Technical know-how	Low	Low	Low
10. Domestic sales	Average/ high	High	Average/ high
11. Foreign sales	Low	High	Average/ high
12. Goodwill	Average	Average	Average
13. Introduction of capital	Low	N/A	Average
14. Remittance of profits	High	N/A	High
15. Repatriation of capital	High	N/A	High

N/A – not applicable

Transport equipment (4.) is a more difficult case; under 'Political action' we have put 'Average' because much transport equipment such as ships or aircraft can be moved in a matter of hours and government action effectively forestalled. Road or rail transport and pipelines are in a different category. Under 'Financial' we have put 'Low' because inflation, devaluation, credit restrictions and so on are likely to leave transportation facilities physically and operationally unaffected.

An oil company, for example, will have such large assets in the high 'political' risk area – land, buildings, manufacturing equipment, raw materials and working capital – that where this type of risk is important it must take special precautions. On the other hand, its foreign sales, which will frequently be much larger than its sales in the local market, will be relatively safe if supplies can be obtained from other sources. Its vulnerability in regard to transport equipment, a major factor in its economy, will probably not be high (unless pipelines are included in this heading). A natural policy to follow will therefore be:

Reduce the value of permanent installations to the minimum.

Spread them over several countries if possible (eg, separate mining from refining).

Use local services extensively.

Base maritime transport equipment on 'safe' ports.

Hold minimum working capital locally.

Have alternative sources of supply to cover foreign sales.

In a 'high-risk' area it might contemplate some sharing of ownership with local interests, as is RTZ's policy, but this raises questions of a different order which will be discussed under the heading of 'ownership policies'.

The history of the oil industry, at least since the Mexican confiscations, has been rather a stormy one, but it has not been unsuccessful in responding to the weakness of its position. Its more recent history, perhaps seen differently by the producing countries, is really a dialectical struggle between its will to survive and expand and the efforts of the producing countries to extract more revenue and achieve more control.

In oil-producing countries the handsome buildings of the 'majors' are part of the local landscape. More discrete but also more numerous are the foreign pharmaceutical companies, with quite a different risk profile. It could easily be deduced from their numbers in even under-developed and 'high-risk' locations that their rating was low on nearly all counts. Fixed assets are generally limited to small buildings with mixing and filling equipment, the operation being based on the importation of finished or semi-finished products. Unit values are low, so the requirement for working capital is low. The only high-risk features of the picture are:

● raw materials, generally imported;

● government licensing or regulation;

● remittance of profits.

The importation of raw materials or semi-finished products may be affected by balance-of-payments difficulties, giving rise to import licensing.

Government licensing exists in most countries but may be used in a discriminatory way against foreign products. Direct government intervention has occurred in Great Britain in the case of a number of products made by foreign companies; this has taken the form of regulation of prices and also importation of products from companies infringing or ignoring the patents of the originators. This is a rather extreme form of action not paralleled in many countries. It is a consequence of success, however, as foreign products had come to represent a large percentage of the purchases, direct or indirect, of the British National Health Service.

It may be interesting to look at a case of a different kind where the risks are high. If one takes a fertilizer-manufacturing company, for example, this is a company with high vulnerability to risk overall, because of heavy capital investment; working capital, because of seasonal factors, will tend to be very high and the turnover will frequently be heavily concentrated in the local market. Such an organization will tend to have a high overall vulnerability under all the three headings.

In a particular situation, which to an oil company, for example, would present a high political risk exposure, the fertilizer business may well have a much lower exposure, although its 'vulnerability index' may be just as high. In fact the uncertainty elements are likely to be quite low, unlike the oil company, but the overall risk exposure will remain high with virtually none of the advantages which the oil company will have. Moreover, and this is a factor which is inseparable from any discussion of risk, the opportunity for profit may be much lower. It is not therefore surprising that foreign-owned fertilizer plants are as uncommon in the world as foreign-owned oil companies are common.

Risk minimizing – the reduction of vulnerability
Although not necessarily by any very systematic or logical process, the company will have reached some general overall concept of its vulnerability to risk. In the case of a particular country it will have given some sort of rating for risks of particular types, perhaps as broad as 'politically sound but prone to inflation'. At this stage, apparently, most companies will be most strongly influenced by their policy as regards market position, largely ignoring any elements that are not too obviously unfavourable. A sizeable and certainly growing proportion however then seek to reduce vulnerability to the key factors.

A risk profile
By giving itself a rating under the three main headings set out, a business can outline a kind of risk profile which in practice will frequently look rather different from the picture obtained by less analytical methods. The picture will apply to all situations which are broadly similar, that is to say, the risk profile will be very similar for all operations of a broadly similar kind, irrespective of the particular environment. An automobile company, for example, will have plants assembling vehicles from, say, 60% locally produced parts and 40% imported parts in six different countries. Irrespective of the characteristics of the country, the risk profile will apply. It will be shown to be

vulnerable in the same respects in all these countries. If the operation is car manufacture from 40% home-produced parts and 60% locally bought in, then the way in which it is vulnerable will be quite different, in degree if not in kind.

TABLE B

VULNERABILITY

	Political action	Commercial risks	Financial risks
1. Land	10	5	3
2. Buildings	10	3	3
3. Manufacturing equipment	10	5	3
4. Transport equipment	4	5	6
5. Raw materials	10	5	6
6. Working capital	10	5	6
7. Skilled staff	0	5	5
8. Labour	5	5	7
9. Technical know-how	2	0	0
10. Domestic sales	2	6	5
11. Foreign sales	0	6	5
12. Goodwill	0	5	0
13. Introduction of capital	0	N/A	5
14. Remittance of profits	0	N/A	2
15. Repatriation of capital	10	N/A	8
	73	55	64

N/A – not applicable

It may be a useful exercise to put values against the different factors, say 1–10, and produce a kind of vulnerability index. The above table attempts to rate the vulnerability of an oil company subsidiary, producing oil but having only limited internal sales. This pattern, as we said earlier, will be more or less valid for all similar operations, irrespective of the country. We can then apply the same technique to the countries, rating them for vulnerability under the three main headings of 'political', 'commercial' and 'financial' risks. This table would be as follows:

TABLE C

	Political	Commercial	Financial
Country A	10	4	3
Country B	2	8	5
Country C	6	5	8

Country A might be, for example, Libya, where the political risk to an oil company would have to be rated as very high; commercial risk probably below average and financial risks rather low because, apart from political action, the financial situation appears at the time of writing to be quite satisfactory.

If these weights are then applied to the vulnerability index a third table can be produced:

TABLE D

	Political	Commercial	Financial
Country A	730	220	192
Country B	146	490	320
Country C	438	275	572

No scientific validity at all can be claimed for this simple piece of methodology, as the values in both Table B and Table C are nothing more than quantifications of the unquantifiable, but the technique is not without value; it focuses attention on the detail of the situation and breaks it down into specific components. As we are using fifteen factors in the vulnerability index the resulting country indices in Table D are an advance on merely impressionistic assessment. There is scope for more refined methods, and major multi-national corporations are researching actively in this field.

Dr Clapham of ICI reports using a somewhat similar technique:

But it is the third step which is the most critical, and this is to assess your list of countries in terms of risk, and to balance the risks against the probable rewards. At this stage you have to look on the operation just as an investment trust manager does when he apportions his funds. As an investor, however, your position is different from his in two ways. First, he can sell out a lot more easily than you can, so that he can sometimes afford greater risks. On the other hand, you may be able to get rewards other than from the dividend of an overseas company, a point we will come to later.

Risks involved

What are the risks to consider? The first is the risk of loss of your investment altogether, by war, revolution, or expropriation without compensation. There are places where these things happen. Secondly, there is the risk of a country's economy becoming chaotic, either making business impossible or making the value of the currency that can be remitted negligible: this disability may or may not be permanent. And finally, there is the risk of various political actions which can reduce the value of an investment materially but not necessarily permanently: devaluation, penal taxation, blocking of remittances of capital or income, price control which makes operation unprofitable, and so on.

To give a numerical value to the risks of investing in any one country is almost impossible, but a convenient way of stating your conclusions is to put against each country the number of years for which you regard its economy – and its politics – as reasonably safe. One simple method is to classify countries into groups for risk purposes: for example, you could take five-year periods and decide which look reasonably safe against the risks I've mentioned for five years, for ten years, for fifteen years and for twenty years: beyond twenty years visibility is low, and in any case by then your plant will normally be fully depreciated.

If you do this, you end up with a list of the countries of the world in which your company could reasonably invest – a list, incidentally, which you must revise at least once a year – graded into four classes of risk. The next thing is to decide what is the maximum proportion of your shareholders' funds which you can reasonably allocate to each category. This is a decision which cannot be taken without knowledge of the compensating rewards, a question we shall be coming to under 'evaluation'.*

An example of risk appraisal

The situation of an oil company might be the following:

Political – very high, say of total risk exposure 70%, for all the reasons mentioned (xenophobia, acquisitiveness, and so on).

Commercial – low. If the operation is basically crude production then the risks will be the normal risks of the area. There may be special risks if the oil is, for example, a particular type for which the demand is fluctuating, or if the economics of production are marginal, making exploitation profitable only in certain situations of market supply.

The market will probably be largely external, so it cannot be affected by local government action, and the company will probably have alternative sources of supply.

Financial – probably relatively low because no large amounts of working capital will be required *internally* in the country, the operation not being labour intensive, and the essential raw material not being purchased. Much expensive plant will be required to be imported in many cases, but the company in such circumstances will be an important earner of foreign exchange, and there will normally not be great difficulty in obtaining the necessary imported supplies.

Financial risks on the whole are likely to be of relatively small importance internally, although changes in exchange rates and taxation may affect the market situation.

We come then to the interesting conclusion that as far as non-political risks are concerned the exposure of an oil-

* Michael J. S. Clapham, *Planning and Managing an Overseas Business* (British Institute of Management).

producing subsidiary of a 'major' is probably much less than normal for the country. The risks are mainly those arising from selective and discriminatory political action.

If the particular country concerned, say Libya or Peru, has a record of political interference, then the high political rating of the country, combined with the high *'political vulnerability'* rating of the business, make an explosive mixture with a low flash point. There may indeed be something in the reflection that such a relatively high degree of invulnerability to many local circumstances may itself engender considerable irritation in government circles.

Of course, while we may recognize that there are grounds for the suspicions and irritations of the local governments, we should not think that the difficulties of the oil companies have necessarily been overstated, since the fact that their overall *risk vulnerability* is so largely political in nature means that it is not risk at all but *uncertainty* which is the main component of their situation.

In discussing a risk policy it is useful to recall that every business has certain objectives in conformity with the nature of the business itself. This will entail doing or being involved in a large number of subsidiary activities which are not central to the business purpose. In a badly managed business there is frequently confusion about the activities, ie,

(a) the activities central to the business;

(b) the activities flowing from (a) but not central to it.

For example, a company whose business is manufacturing insecticides may also:

spray crops for customers;

operate aircraft for the purpose.

There will also be a wide range of other risks which we incur because they arise as secondary consequences of our policies.

The first we may call 'voluntary risks', the second 'involuntary risks'. A mining company which sets out to explore in a given territory calculates what the risks of failure may be; it has certain general statistics to guide it, and certain information specifically about the territory. It may reach the conclusion that it has a one-in-four chance of finding what it seeks, and its risk exposure is consequently quantifiable in money terms.

At the same time it has to incur a whole range of involuntary risks, in most cases related to the environment in which it is operating – government policies, taxation, even the risk of expropriation.

The attitude to the voluntary risks will be that they are incurred in the hope of compensatory gain. Frequently they are risks in the exact sense of the word, that is to say that success can be calculated within a range of probabilities.

Moreover, one man's uncertainty is another man's risk; we have discussed briefly the attitude of the exporter who will accept the commercial risk of the transaction but wishes to off-load the currency risk on to someone else. This is because he is skilled in the interpretation of the commercial risk, but not the currency risk. The foreign-exchange dealers, however, specialize in the risks and evaluate them within very narrow limits. They represent uncertainty to the exporter but risk to the exchange dealer.

In many situations there will therefore be:

● risk situations, as viewed by the initiator of the project;

● risk situations which are uncertainty situations to him but risk situations to another skilled in the evaluation of these particular risks;

● general uncertainty situations which cannot be reduced to 'risk' situations.

The initiator of the project will therefore look first at the risks which are central to his project and which, more or less by definition, he is skilled in interpreting.

On the second-order risks, perhaps in the case of our mining project – matters of currency, and so on – he will consult the best authorities, local and international bankers.

The uncertainty factors he will seek to evaluate qualitatively by seeking information in all possible quarters. There may frequently be political risks, concerned more with unquantifiable social factors than with economic matters.

What is important in the decision-making process is that the *relative* importance of the 'risk' and 'uncertainty' factors should be appraised; the tendency will be to overestimate the uncertainty factors and to treat them independently of the risk factors. The fact that the risk factors can be quantified will tend to make them appear less important, whereas in fact they may be much more important than the uncertainty factors, and the risk evaluation may be very inaccurate. It is quite common for a project which has extremely broad assumptions about, for example, selling prices, to be treated as an exercise in political judgement. It would be more appropriate to spend more time determining the range of probabilities in the selling-price estimates and giving less to the uncertainties.

It is undoubtedly this instinctive feeling for the difference between 'risk' and 'uncertainty' situations which leads to the magnifying of the political risks; it is felt that an outsider can form some reasonable judgement about quantifiable situations such as costs or even marketing possibilities, whereas, rightly, it is recognized that to deal with the 'uncertainty' elements, particularly social and political, an intimate personal acquaintance with the situation is indispensable.

Academic writers on international business are inclined to stress the importance of forecasting 'environmental adversities', political or economic. One of the most recent and competent works on financial management is critical of an executive of a multi-national corporation who is quoted as saying: 'We don't try to forecast, we just try to be prepared.' Certainly, if the speaker meant that they took no interest in the possibility of unfavourable events, then obviously that is not an intelligent attitude, but it is almost certain that he did not. His comment would be a fairly typical one on the part of a responsible executive, because *forecasting* such complex phenomena as devaluation or political change would only be undertaken in order to make a specific plan; otherwise the only course of action is 'to be prepared', in other words, to be more or less permanently in a 'least-risk' posture. To alter policies according to forecasts of such complex possibilities would be to expose the business to additional risks in an area where the businessman would have no particular competence. The professional risk-bearer – foreign-exchange dealer, insurance institution – has to make forecasts, but he also possesses a particular skill in evaluating risks, laying them off to other risk-bearers in a way which is not possible to the ordinary company. Some of the very largest corporations have found it worth while to be in the risk-bearing business themselves by owning insurance companies, as they might own advertising agencies, but this is another story entirely.

Operating a business on a 'siege' basis, that is, with all its defences ready, a 'low-risk profile', and so on, is frequently a frustrating and expensive method, and in consequence it is important for local events to be followed very carefully, and extra precautions taken from time to time, but on the whole our experience tends to be rather in the direction of the executive quoted, following events closely, not relying too much on forecasting unless it is to raise or lower the defences a little. It is not so much that the trend of events cannot be forecast – it frequently can – but that the timing is so difficult to calculate in any meaningful terms that the forecasts are virtually useless. We remember rather vividly an extremely well-documented and thoughtful study on the position of the dollar that came to our desk in 1963; it forecast an early devaluation. The writer returned it to the president of the company with the brief comment that it was an extremely interesting study but that the dollar would not be devalued. The fact was that the conditions normally tending to force devaluation already existed in those far-off days, but the United States had no basic interest in the raising of the price of gold and would therefore resist such a move by every means in its power, and, as was to be seen later, those means were not few. In summary, the best policy would appear to be to follow events closely, taking the best advice possible; maintain a 'low-risk' posture if there is reason, restricting specific forecasts to those which *must* be made. By the last phrase we mean that certain decisions will *imply* a forecast; for example, the decision to buy land for a plant instead of leasing it will carry certain implications about relative costs versus relative risks, for example of expropriation, and in this case there is no way of avoiding a forecast; the only question is whether the forecast is *implicit* or *explicit*. It has some chance of being a better forecast if it is explicit, that is, thought out in advance, based on stated assumptions and following a definite line of reasoning. The advantage of the explicit forecast is that it can be checked periodically and changed if, for example, the basic assumptions no longer apply. If it is implicit, the reasons why it was made will soon be forgotten, and the process of re-evaluation, if it is done at all, will be that much more difficult.

We think it is considerations of the foregoing order, not obscurantism, which explain the rather sharp cleavage which appears frequently to exist between the business executive and the academic writer, and which the comment quoted epitomizes.

More sophisticated risk-evaluation

Much more sophisticated techniques than those described are beginning to come into use, not only in connexion with international business. The assessment of capital projects in general leaves a good deal to be desired if it is based on a static model; both alternative assumptions and the relative probability of a particular outcome need to be introduced to enable different alternatives to be evaluated.

A recent writer on international business, Robert B. Stobaugh Jr, of the Harvard Business School, discusses risk analysis in relation to the economic and political stability of a foreign country:

After considering a number of approaches to this task, such as go–no go, premium for risk, and range of estimates, he discusses the application of risk analysis:

> In the case of devaluation, we would assess the probability of devaluation in each time period (for example, each year) and the probability of the amount of devaluation in each of these time periods. Thus in year one we might estimate a .100 probability of devaluation. Of this .100, we might estimate a .025 for a 15 percent devaluation, a .050 probability for a 20 percent devaluation, and a .025 probability for a 25 percent devaluation. Similarly, we would estimate probabilities for the other important variables, and then use a [Monte Carlo] simulation to obtain a distribution of the probable results.

> Mr Stobaugh shows how a risk curve can be drawn for the final result measure that is used to evaluate an investment. Another of the particular questions he feels is suitable for analysis using the risk analysis technique is the threat of nationalization of a plant once built. In all these cases, the decision maker is aided by having a risk distribution to consider rather than a single best estimate.*

There is a wide range of techniques available: probability theory, Bayesian analysis, decision trees, and so on. Computer simulations are being used extensively with simple models such as we have discussed, the values for the variables being changed to see what the overall effect is.

How far are these techniques useful in practice? Certainly the more sophisticated mathematical techniques involve so much work that their use cannot be justified in other than major situations. Secondly, the techniques require a large number of assumptions to be made, and can only show the effect of adopting certain assumptions – they cannot be more accurate than the basic material. In many situations there is

* Ernest C. Miller, *Advanced Techniques for Strategic Planning* (American Management Association). Reprinted by permission of the publisher.

true uncertainty and this by definition cannot be effectively quantified.

In summary, then, an orderly appraisal of the main factors, such as we have outlined, will normally be found sufficient because in the last analysis it is more the examination of the situation than the results of the analysis which is valuable in the present state of knowledge:

> One foundation of the analytical approach we developed in the Pentagon was the notion of open and explicit analysis. By that I mean that all criteria, assumptions, calculations, empirical data, and judgments should be described in the analysis in such a way that they can be subjected to checking, testing, criticising, debate, discussion, and possible refutation. The explanation of the method of calculation should be detailed enough to allow other investigators to reproduce the results. A really good analysis will be self-explanatory and, ideally, will help a person with a different point of view to understand how he might reasonably reach different conclusions if he believes different assumptions. Openness and explicitness gives an analysis a certain self-correcting character: it is our best protection against persistence in error. Moreover, open and explicit analysis builds confidence in the results and in the decisions based on the analysis.*

The present writer, in so far as most problems are concerned, would agree with the following statement:

> These quantitative techniques are too much. I am not at all sure that the payoff from using the techniques is proportionate to the cost. Many of our operating people disregard efforts to use them. I think all the techniques are valuable as paradigms for thought, but they are tools to achieve an end rather than ends in themselves. Unfortunately, those who are expert in the techniques often seem to take a different view.†

---

* A. Harvey, *Factors Making for Implementation Success and Failure*, as quoted by Ernest C. Miller, op cit.
† As quoted by Ernest C. Miller, op cit.

The form of establishment and ownership policies

In this discussion we have referred a number of times to the sharing of ownership with local interests as a means of conciliating nationalistic or local antagonisms. The policies of RTZ in mining ventures have been contrasted, for example, with those of most of the major American and British oil companies.

The issue is, however, a wider one than that of economic nationalism. As we have seen (Chapter 5), what is sold in the international market may be anything from an idea to hardware, each described as the same 'product'. Coca-Cola, to take an example to which we are somewhat addicted, is a trade mark, an essence, a marketing concept and even a soft drink in a bottle.

If this general proposition is true, then the originator of the 'product' has a variety of choice about what he will sell abroad, and how he will sell it. He may license some domestic firm to export the product; he may exploit it in collaboration with a foreign company – he has in short a very great range of possibilities in most cases: which he chooses is determined by a wide range of policy and operating considerations, including finance, manpower and the local situation.

One of the major considerations in his choice is the question of risk. We will therefore enumerate briefly the different ways in which he may operate, with some of the advantages and disadvantages of each. Our discussion will be primarily concerned with the risk factor, but we should say once and for all that this is only one of a wide variety of considerations in determining the final choice. In some situations it will, however, be the determining factor.

Licensing

From some aspects this represents the minimum risk exposure, since no assets other than know-how are located in the foreign country. The risk may be, however, that the royalties will not be paid under various pretexts (or under none at all), and that the territory will not be respected. It is unlikely that the foreign company will have adequate protection everywhere and the licensee may take advantage of the fact to go outside the agreed territory. This type of arrangement gives rise in practice to serious disagreements. Apart from a number of obvious commercial disadvantages, a licensing arrangement may involve serious political risks.

Management contracts

This is an arrangement whereby the foreign company supplies services, which may or may not include technical knowledge, in exchange for an annual fee. It is in practice quite common in airline operation and hotel management, although in the latter case the arrangement is made for normal commercial reasons, hotels being built by property developers who have no particular knowledge of the hotel business.

It was an arrangement popular in India before independence, when agency firms were appointed as 'managing agents' for British firms not wishing to sever their connexions with their distributors, or for other reasons.

It offers virtually total security to the foreign firm, but in general has little appeal to major undertakings since it is not permanent and does not generally employ more than a section of the company's resources. It is frequently suggested that it is likely to expand very much in the future, but the evidence for this is not strong at the present time. If it does it will certainly in part be as an offset to the political influence of the socialist countries, which are frequently interested in operations of this type.

Joint ventures

The joint venture may be either 50/50, a majority or minority participation, and the terms on which each partner participates need not be the same. The local partner may, for example, subscribe for shares in cash, the foreign partner in exchange for know-how, market position or some other non-monetary consideration. From a commercial point of view most foreign companies seek a controlling interest, but clearly this has many of the disadvantages of a wholly-owned undertaking, from a political point of view, while having a number of the commercial disadvantages of a partnership. In many cases the most satisfactory position is a minority position without a corresponding cash stake.

In practice the risk exposure of these various courses of action has to be assessed compared with the extent to which they protect the market position. For example, an arrangement in Japan may be made with a local producer, as has in the immediate post-war period been almost mandatory. This may be financially satisfactory in so far as the foreign company may have some equity participation in the venture, and it may indeed have other advantages such as royalties for know-how and profits from the supply of products. It may therefore have secured all the advantages of direct participation in the market, in so far as its immediate profit position is concerned, while its additional risk exposure, resulting from its equity participation, may be quite small, since apart from the smallness of the amount, the investment may be sound in itself. Its original objective may not however have been completely achieved since control of this market position will have passed to a company in which it is a minority shareholder. It is not unusual in such cases for the minority shareholder to find that other products are substituted for its own; the value of the know-how it has contributed is progressively eroded; and it finally becomes, for better or for worse, the owner of a minority position in a company which has little to do with its own business and which no longer fulfils the purpose for which it was created. This is a common example of a situation where a risk-minimizing policy designed to protect an asset has failed to achieve its objective and more exposure to risk would have been justified.

Obviously all these arrangements are pursued largely, although not exclusively, because of their risk-minimizing aspects. There are frequent cases where there is a real community of interest.

Consortia or groups

The consortium or group may be national or multi-national. In the case of the national consortium the principal advantage to each participant may be that foreign control is preserved while the share of each is reduced to what are, presumably, acceptable proportions. The arrangement is not likely to be much more acceptable to the host country than control by a single foreign firm, that is, unless one or more of the participants is well known in the host country and has an outstandingly good record in their eyes.

The multi-national consortium is obviously a very different animal, and may have the advantage of deterring hostile action by enlarging the number of countries which may be offended thereby. This type of consortium tends perhaps to be rather commoner in ex-colonial territories, when the former colonial power wishes to be associated with a more neutral partner. The most important consortium of recent years is probably the successor to the Anglo-Iranian Oil Company in managing the Abadan Refinery. There are a number of international oil consortia as well as mining companies. It is not an arrangement favoured by manufacturing companies, for rather obvious reasons.

Partnership with government

This is a rather special form of association which theoretically should offer a high degree of security against political action, unless there is a radical change of government. It is in effect the only form of operation open to foreign firms in Eastern European countries such as Yugoslavia, Rumania, Hungary and Poland. It has no value independently of the contractual arrangements made at the time of the formation of the 'company'. These may provide for the remuneration of the capital and its repatriation in certain stated eventualities.

There is a strong trend in the less developed countries particularly for governments to seek to obtain some equity stake. At the present time great pressure is being brought to bear on the oil companies by OPEC (Organization of Petroleum Exporting

Countries) to obtain varying degrees of partnership with the marketing companies. In many cases they have succeeded and one of the latest and most interesting instances is reported as follows:

Peru's nationalist military regime which came to power three years ago, confiscating the operation and assets of a United States oil giant, has in the last six months achieved a remarkable investment breakthrough. A set of new 'model' oil exploration contracts have been eagerly signed by 10 North American and two British oil companies . . .

The most significant aspect of the 'Peruvian model' contracts and the reason why more than a dozen American and European oil companies have suddenly 'joined the queue' lies in the terms the US Occidental Petroleum Corporation obtained when it signed Petroperu's first contract last June.

They marked a new breakthrough of realism by the regime: after its nationalist phase it has now settled down to a rational effort to attract foreign capital on modern terms.

Peru's revolutionary government has still paid no compensation to the International Petroleum Company, a Standard Oil of New Jersey subsidiary. The regime decided back in 1969 that the concession system was a thing of the past.

Under the Peruvian model contract, all oil found by foreign companies is Peruvian. It will go to Petroperu which will 'pay back' Occidental, for instance, at the well head on a 50:50 basis for its services – exploration, investment, running costs, etc – plus, in the event of oil being found, a 'reasonable profit' as the official decree puts it.

The bulk of the company's taxes and royalties will fall to be paid by Petroperu to the Peruvian state out of the state concern's share of the oil. The foreign companies are assured their right to sell the oil obtained on world markets, after supplying certain limited local needs, and guaranteed that profits can be remitted in foreign currency despite Peru's tough exchange restrictions.

The companies are committed in turn to a four year

exploration period, drilling three wells, and a possible extension at the rate of a well drilling every five months for a subsequent three year period – all without direct financial cost to Peru.

The subsequent contracts, all for 35 years (including British Petroleum's) were signed after the Peruvian authorities had got over their surprise at the welcome response from world oil circles. They include a percentage share out which benefits Petroperu as production rises – 50:50 for the first 100,000 barrels per day, 49:51 up to 200,000 and 48:52 from then on . . .

A 'supervisory committee' (including Petroperu officials and the Peruvian armed forces) will have the task of seeing that the foreign companies keep the contracts.*

Local branch or subsidiary company

In recent years this has tended to be the chosen vehicle of the largest corporations. The subsidiary company, incorporated normally with limited liability in the foreign country, may have local shareholdings, and at one time this arrangement was not unusual: English Ford, H. J. Heinz in England and more recently RTZ in Australia and Canada are well-known examples. For reasons which will be discussed the trend has been against local participation in more recent times.

The wholly-owned foreign subsidiary is a rather curious phenomenon. By being incorporated under local laws it has the protection afforded by limited liability; it can be liquidated by the parent company and default on its local debts. Its creditors to some extent at least will have put their faith in the international, not the local, company, and may therefore be legitimately disappointed. When the time of liquidation comes it may be found that the assets are chiefly owned by the parent company, often through current account and supply arrangements.

Then, while it may have to file accounts and make tax

* 'Peruvian Contracts open up prospects for new oil deals', *The Times*, January 26th, 1972.

returns, these are frequently meaningless since a large proportion of the transactions in question may not be of a 'normal' nature and distortions of various kinds may have been introduced to limit tax liability or for other reasons. In short, it may seem to the local government concerned to be a somewhat unequal arrangement in which the chief advantages rest with the foreign controlling interest.

Ownership policies

There are very strong forces pulling in the direction of local control of the operations of international companies. Requirements regarding the employment of local nationals, participation in capital, and so on, are not new, but with the rapid growth of multi-national enterprise, particularly American, many countries, and not only the less developed ones, have felt the need to allow something less than total freedom to the stranger. Even in the United States, too, there have been powerful opponents of the 'new imperialism', and pleaders for partnership with the 'host' country. A well-known work, *International Business Policy*,* has put the case in detail and with considerable persuasive force.

The risks of government intervention and regulation in the seventies are probably in general greater than they were and constitute a serious hazard to the operations abroad of the multi-national company. The reasons for this stem both from the situation of the host country and from the growing size, power and integration of many multi-national companies.

The risks of interference have always been quite considerable and are growing greater rather than the reverse. These risks are not, in general, being met by an accommodating attitude on the part of many companies, who are resolutely sticking to their policies of total ownership. They do not see in the alternative policies so much an opportunity to reduce risk as the likelihood that it will be increased, or at least that the disadvantages will be so great that the alternatives cannot be

* R. D. Robinson, *International Business Policy* (Holt, Rinehart and Winston).

considered. The matter could not be more clearly stated than it has by Frederic G. Donner, Chairman of General Motors Corporation:

In General Motors we have tried to keep these facts constantly in mind while at the same time exploring new ways to assure that our activities are closely identified with the development of each national economy in which we operate. To this end, I established in 1960 a National Identification Committee to make a continuing reexamination of our overseas operating policies and positions. The Committee members – top officers from the Overseas Division and the central office staff – completed their first report to the Board of Directors in 1961.

That report was based upon a careful review of the changing nature of our operations outside the United States and the changing nature of the world environment. It included summaries of surveys covering a wide range of subjects such as national attitudes toward investment by United States companies, the approach of firms in the United States to overseas investment, employment and ownership policy.

I will touch on three of the Committee's recommendations, reserving for the next chapter a more thorough examination of their implementation.

First, it was concluded that our long-standing policy of maintaining complete ownership of our operating subsidiaries was essential to the efficient world operation of General Motors, and remained as compelling as it had ever been. During the postwar period, the forces of world competition in motor vehicles had greatly intensified with advancing industrialization. The world, particularly the Western world, was moving toward much closer economic ties. National markets were being consolidated into larger regional markets in Europe and South America, and in North America already close ties were being strengthened. In our view, these basic trends toward integration of product markets reinforced the requirements of a unified ownership point of view.

Second, the Committee found a growing desire in many countries for ownership participation in General Motors and its subsidiaries. This desire, I might add, had been made very clear to me in conversations with government and business leaders overseas . . .

Closely related to the General Motors incentive compensation plan is our policy of a unified ownership of overseas subsidiaries. Both follow logically from the inherent interdependence of our divisions and subsidiaries around the world. From an operational point of view, our overseas subsidiaries are as fully integrated in our overall operations as any division or plant in the United States. The fact that an overseas subsidiary is governed by the regulations of another sovereign nation does not alter this basic business relationship. Nor does the particular location of the operation in any way diminish the need for a coordinated approach to serving world markets. On the contrary, geographical dispersion makes the need for coordination even more compelling.

The strategic importance of a unified ownership of operating units was recognized at a very early stage in the development of General Motors overseas. A policy of coordinated control could be expected to result in improved business efficiency only if it had as its counterpart a policy of unified ownership. And as we have accumulated world-wide operating experience, our view on unified ownership has been strongly reinforced.*

Natural-resources companies

The natural-resources companies are exposed to even greater dangers of this kind since they are seen to be actually taking the country's wealth out of the ground and exporting it. These resources have finite lives, and this makes the situation even more acute. The Shah of Persia referred, in the confrontation

* Frederic G. Donner, *The World-Wide Industrial Enterprise* (McGraw-Hill).

of 1971 between OPEC and the oil companies, to this fact. In general, however, the oil companies have pursued policies of 100% ownership and basically for the same reasons as General Motors. In recent years these policies, as we have shown, have had to be modified under pressure.

A different attitude has been that of Rio Tinto Zinc, expressed as follows by Mr Roy Wright:

> When we start in a new territory, we always discuss with the local government our general philosophy and explain in depth how we shall proceed, so that there can be no misunderstanding. Often we seek modifications to existing tax or royalty laws, and occasionally, in those countries where large-scale mining has not previously been known, we help draft new legislation to put that particular country on a par with other important mining countries. This we accept as a major responsibility because governments come and go but we cannot move our mine, so the mining tax laws we ask for must not only be fair and sensible to the host country and to us, but must be understood to be so by reasonable politicians of all shades and to the population generally. If we are welcomed by the government, we set up a 100% owned company and then form below that another company known as the local national company.
>
> This second company then proceeds to carry out the exploration work. We have always believed it wise not to involve the local population financially during this high risk period, though we might, as I have mentioned, invite other international partners or local mining companies to share this risk with us. If we are successful then the project is hived off and becomes an operating mining company, in which our shareholding is held through our local national company. At some future date the mining company usually goes public – assuming, of course, that the country has a stock market – and occasionally the local government takes a shareholding in this company. We continue to expand in this way, creating new operating mining companies, usually all with

different shareholders, until the time comes when our local national company, which holds our shareholding in the various operating companies, can also go public . . .

One fundamental part of our philosophy is that the UK parent company must not restrict the planned and healthy growth of the national company, even if for some reason we could not follow a share issue. Such a situation has not yet arisen, although both in Australia and elsewhere we have deliberately refrained from taking up our shares as part of our policy of letting the local population have a bigger stake in the national company.

Obviously, when we initially move into a new territory, London headquarters carries the entire technical, financial and administrative burden, but as the local company grows, so we shed more and more responsibility, until what one might describe as a directly controlled colony reaches self-government and becomes totally identified with the local scene.

The national parent company must, in our view, be truly national and so the Chairman and Chief Executive is a man of national stature and repute, such as Sir Maurice Mawby in Australia. Further, we believe that the senior staff, both administrative and technical, as well as a preponderance of the Board, should, wherever possible, be local nationals. Obviously, in the developing territories and in those countries where we start *ab initio*, this is not always possible, but again our aim is quite clear and we set out deliberately to recruit or train local nationals to take responsibility at all levels as quickly as possible. Not only do we believe this is right from a national viewpoint and in identifying our local company with the country, but it is the only way whereby we can retain a relatively small number of highly qualified men on the London headquarters payroll who can move from country to country to deal with specific and urgent problems beyond the experience of the local team.*

* Roy W. Wright, *The Policies and Practices of the Rio Tinto Zinc Corporation Ltd*, 1968.

In the latter case, however, the situation is somewhat different inasmuch as the mining company does not process and distribute finished products, at least only to a minor extent. The degree of integration of the various operations is much lower than in the other cases discussed.

Acquisition

Frequently, after considering the alternatives discussed, such as joint ventures, licensing, etc, a company will decide that the purchase of a local base will serve its interests better and will provide it particularly with the local operating know-how without which investment in the market represents too great a hazard. Many major corporations have expanded in this way: General Motors, with the purchase of Vauxhall Motors in England and Adam Opel in Germany; Olivetti, with the purchase of Underwood Typewriter in the USA; Rhône Poulenc with the purchase of May and Baker in England.

The objective may be many-sided, arising from one or more of the motives discussed, but particularly from the desire to acquire experience without the risk of a long period of trial and error and gradual adaptation to the environment. We have quoted Mr Sloan of General Motors, referring to their attempts to make acquisitions in Germany, France and England.

The case of W. R. Grace has been mentioned. Grace already had very important manufacturing and selling interests in Europe, mainly concerned with chemicals and plastic wrappings. The food business was a new venture and in conformity with the instinctive behaviour of this, one of the earliest multi-nationals, the parameters of the operation were intended to describe a 'least risk' situation.

● The sectors chosen were to be well established and rather conservative so that the 'learning curve' of the Grace management would be in advance of the changes going on in the industry.

- 'Grass roots' situations, ie, building businesses from scratch, were specifically excluded as requiring too much management and too much time to acquire experience by the usual process of trial and error.

- Acquisitions were to contribute to current earnings, and were not to be 'ailing companies'.

- There was to be a strong assets basis as an insurance against failure.

- The business was to be such that it could be sold if eventually it did not fit in with the desired pattern of the overall operation.

- Management was a *sine qua non*.

- The hundred per cent ownership was to be preferred, but in any case effective managerial and financial control was mandatory.

The risk factor plays an important, perhaps the most important, part in the decision about the form of ownership to be used. Other factors are frequently concerned, such as the availability of capital or management, but the risk factor is almost always present as a major consideration. To experienced operators, however, anything less than 100% ownership frequently represents additional risk, not less.

In the sixties the Ford Motor Company wished to increase the degree of integration of its manufacturing operations and found that the public ownership of a large percentage of shares in the UK company would be likely to limit its freedom of action. It accordingly made an attractive offer for the publicly held shares and thus re-acquired complete ownership. The trend is undoubtedly towards more, not less, international integration of facilities in multi-national corporations and, whatever may be the initial formula of ownership adopted, it is likely to be chosen with a view to change in the direction of greater control, if this is found to be beneficial. There are exceptions, and the opposite policy is followed by RTZ, as Mr Roy Wright has written; they prefer to bear all the initial risks of exploration and proving the mine, only looking to local public subscription when the project is firmly established. This represents a balancing of risks of various kinds, namely that the initial risks represent the expertise of the mining company, so that in effect the value of a proven property will be much higher than that of one which is purely speculative, but the risks of foreign ownership are such as to render it desirable for substantial local capital to be introduced when large-scale extraction and export of minerals is contemplated. If the risks of the exploration stage seem too great they are spread, or 'laid off', by association with other more or less professional risk-takers, ie, mining companies, rather than with the non-professional. Frequently, even very large organizations will 'lay off' risks in this way, preferring not to have all their eggs in one basket if, so to speak, the risk of breakage is too great.

A dynamic situation

We may have seemed to suggest that these decisions are of a once-for-all character; that having decided on the best policy to follow, given the environmental conditions, the decision to adopt one or other form of operation is taken to the exclusion of any other. Of course this is not so, and with every company there is a constant review of conditions; licences expire and so the matter has to be decided *de novo*; the arrangement may not be satisfactory and perhaps the licence is acquired by the licensor; the subsidiary company becomes so large that it is too conspicuous locally and so stock is offered to the investing public, and so on. Far from being static the pattern is constantly shifting from lesser to greater involvement, from indirect to direct participation, and the reverse.

Conclusion

It may perhaps have been noted in the discussion on risks in this and the preceding chapter that more emphasis has been placed on the undoubted fact of risk and the many forms which it can take than on the attitudes of businessmen to it. We have quoted fairly extensively from Dr Clapham of ICI and referred to others in passing, but we have not dealt explicitly with this important question.

Two aspects of the matter will have emerged clearly, however; namely, that the attitude towards risk in the case of particular countries or even whole continents is more emotional than reasoned, and that by 'risk' is generally meant 'uncertainty'; it is this handicap to forward planning that seems frequently to be more important than the risk of loss. Secondly, we think it incontrovertible that the businessman does not consider that his profit is a recompense for skilfully calculating and bearing serious risk; on the contrary he regards his profits as the legitimate reward for skill in buying and selling, manufacturing, innovation, or indeed in a complex of factors. In other words, he is not in the risk-bearing business, but equally he is not unprepared to run normal commercial risks; his attitude is that of risk minimization. Sometimes he will set his face against risk altogether, and in a survey of the practice of large corporations one respondent stated indeed that his policy was to avoid risk. On the other side, corporations firmly wedded to risk minimization will have an occasional 'flutter'; W. R. Grace, for example, took part in an oil-drilling consortium in Libya at the beginning of the development of that country's resources, and this very limited excursion into a very high-risk activity was rewarded with success. But these are exceptions, and in general there seems no doubt that risk minimization is the preferred policy.

Unlike risk-bearing, however, this is a negative policy and implies the subordination of risk criteria to some other. There is no universal consensus on what this is, but such research as has been made suggests that the principal motive is a rather elusive concept described as 'market position'. This raises an important question, namely, why this concept has not been discussed in more depth in this examination of the characteristics of international business. It is true that we referred to it in the first chapter, but if we have not devoted more time to it it is because it is in fact a characteristic of all business and does not differ in nature or degree from the concept of market position in a single country. The methods by which it is prosecuted are and have to be different, and will be discussed in detail under the heading of 'international marketing'. The two important facts as regards market position as a concept in international business are: few businesses approach the problem from a positive angle; most, at least as far as investment is concerned, follow a passive or defensive strategy;* and it is risk which in most cases is the restraining force, risks in international business being obviously greater than in domestic. The nature and degree of risk, both in fact and even more as perceived by most businessmen, are different from those in domestic business, and this has therefore seemed to us to be the more characteristic feature.

But all the same, is this emphasis on risk justified? Is it not a negative aspect of business? How can the avoidance or minimization of risk make money? Of course the bearing of risk, the third alternative, can, because it is the basis of all insurance and all speculation, but can risk minimization? These are important questions if we are postulating, as this writer has done, that risk is one of the most important and most characteristic elements of international business.

Surely the answer is to be found, as it frequently is, in the most fundamental reactions of the body? The avoidance of risk cannot provide food, shelter, warmth or any of the basic requirements of man for survival, but man and every other

---

* For example:
'Before the group sailed I gave Mr Smith a formal memorandum outlining the situation as I saw it. I asked him to bear these questions in mind:

... Is there not an opportunity for the Corporation to protect its large organization, large volume and substantially large profits accruing to it through its Continental and English operations and, to some extent, afford protection to its overseas business elsewhere by investing capital in manufacturing abroad and making a substantial return on that additional capital?'
Alfred P. Sloan Jr, *My Years with General Motors* (Pan).

creature is provided with a highly sensitive apparatus for perceiving and evaluating risk; his body is in a permanent state of alert as anyone can verify in, for example, an aircraft – at the slightest sign of any abnormality perceived even by the subconscious the whole body is awakened to the possible danger. Then man – and many other animals – has an almost instantaneous means of mobilizing the defences, in man through the injection of adrenalin into the blood stream, so that his maximum capabilities are ready for fight or flight.

This sensory apparatus and the response mechanisms are essential to survival, just as the awareness of risk, and the means of evaluating it and responding to it, are in business.

Conclusion

I quoted in the introduction a passage from Professor Vernon ending as follows: '... And the pragmatic professional, operating out of a clinical experience that usually involves considerable exposure to uncertainty and risk, often has some difficulty in articulating just what his operating rules may be.'

If you add to the factors of uncertainty and risk certain others which I have judged to be significant also, then Professor Vernon has defined the framework for the study of international business from the standpoint of management. I have, in effect, tried to do exactly this – to define the problem as it presents itself in the real world, and to 'articulate' what the businessman's operating rules may be. I have spent a good deal of time discussing the nature of the problem, and have made a number of important points about it which I think are new, and I have done this in the belief that an understanding of any problem, and the analytical tools to deal with it, are much more important than the solutions. These latter are concerned frequently with narrowly particular circumstances, and if the real nature of the problem is understood, it is not difficult, and certainly more useful and rewarding, to strip away the super-fluities and find the answer. This is not therefore a 'how to do it' book, although at the end of some of the chapters I have summarized the implications of the analysis for practical management.

The importance of the basic analysis is shown, in my judgement, by the fact that except for financial management the subject hardly exists as yet. In conversation recently a senior executive of one of the world's largest multi-national companies was positively scathing about 'international marketing' and other subjects as taught at the present time. The international content, in his view, was minimal. Now, I thought some time ago, before this book was contemplated, that this was due to the lack of a coherent theory of international business, and I still think so after the strenuous and obviously only partially successful attempt to create one. Using the concepts of this book I have indeed found it possible to construct a framework for a theory of international marketing which I think has some practical value, and the same applies to the other main functions of the business.

Perhaps what is more important is what remains to be done; any book which claims to deal with basic issues should raise far more problems than it solves. The poor author leaves his work feeling that he is only at the beginning of it, and the only consolation he can find is that he has revealed interesting and perhaps important problems for others to deal with.

Certainly in some areas such as communications and organization (very closely related, as I have emphasized), there is an enormous amount to be done. Pragmatic solutions, sometimes on quite novel levels, have been found to very complex problems, where indeed the breakdown of very large businesses was threatened, but the theoretical basis of most of this work is very weak indeed. Merely to mention quantification in such a context is to show how far we still are from any satisfactory understanding of the processes we are dealing with.

It will undoubtedly be noted that I have not chosen to share the view of a large number of writers regarding the alleged conflict of interest of host countries with foreign investors. Particularly since the publication of *The American Challenge*,[*] which, however, only restated an old argument in an extreme form, great stress has been laid on this aspect of international business. Obviously in the case of a country such as Canada this is a problem of great significance and in the case of industrially weak countries such as most of those in the Middle East or South America there is undoubtedly much hostility.

This is a fact, and as such some writers such as Professor

[*] J. J. Servan-Schreiber, *Le Défi Américain*.

Fayerweather* have considered it to be a distinguishing feature of international business. It may be so, although it seems to me to be in the same area as the relationship between buyer and seller: the host country either wishes to buy the benefits offered by the foreign investor or it does not; if it does, there is a price at which the transaction will take place, more or less to the satisfaction of both parties. I would place more emphasis on the ways in which this price should be determined than on some supposed conflict between the two parties.

This is indeed the reason why I have not treated this issue as one of the major factors in my analysis. If it is a major factor indeed it is of a politico-economic character and concerns the environment in which the businessman has to operate. I am thus aware of its importance, and indeed anyone who has been concerned in recent years with India, France or some South American countries could not be ignorant of the need to reach an understanding with government. I do not, however, regard it as a universal characteristic of international business influencing the decision-making process of the businessman.

I have discussed the multi-national corporations (in Chapter 2) but I have not laid much stress on this aspect of their operations any more than I would feel the need to discuss the Anti-Trust legislation in the US in a book about management in general. These are questions for the economist rather than the businessman, or indeed the business theorist. They are essentially questions of power and do not become important until they present a challenge either to the State itself or to some policy, such as the importance of competition, to which the State is deeply committed. They are not unimportant questions and the businessman may at times have to take cognizance of them. If he does, he has Professor Vernon (*Sovereignty at Bay*) and the Harvard multi-national corporation project to guide him.

There is another rather notable omission from the discussion which calls for comment. I refer to the 'socialist' economies of

* John Fayerweather, *International Business Management* (McGraw-Hill).

the Eastern bloc, China and Cuba. Not all the details of my analysis are relevant to doing business in these special conditions. The system is still substantially that of State monopoly trading through the medium of specialized agencies; the possibilities of direct investment, that is, where trading, manufacturing and financing are all in the same hands, are still very limited. It is true that some special types of 'joint ventures' are now possible in Yugoslavia, Rumania, Poland and Hungary, but many of the complications I have discussed in relation to subsidiary-company operations simply do not occur because this form of organization does not exist. It is indeed a little difficult to see how the freedom of capitalist enterprise can be reconciled with detailed State planning, but one cannot really exclude any possibility after seeing the developments which have occurred in the last ten years.

The essential process common to most 'socialist' countries is the control of all foreign trade by the State organs. The motives governing foreign trade are different from those of the capitalist economies, although there are signs of convergence of aims. At the present time the State planning organs determine how much foreign exchange is likely to be available and this is then allocated to the purchase of goods and services according to several different criteria. In the first place there are essential technological products which are not yet produced in the country concerned, then there are purchases to make up deficiencies in the execution of the plan and, finally, goods which are less essential but considered desirable for particular purposes. Our basic economic law of comparative advantage is not altogether absent in this process, because in fact many of the things which are purchased could be made locally, but at the price of a diversion of effort from more essential products. It may be expected that the importance of comparative advantage will increasingly be recognized as time goes on.

Does our basic analysis apply? Do these transactions exhibit complexity, difficulties in communication and a wider range of risks than domestic transactions? Certainly they do, and there are, for example, special arrangements in most developed countries for insurance in trade with the socialist countries. Of course, if this book were primarily concerned with East/West trade and not with trade in the Western world the details of the analysis would in many cases be different and the examples almost entirely so; it would be necessary to discuss in detail the workings of the State machine since in the last analysis the State is the only customer. It is also a curious paradox which would need examination that while the State in the socialist economies has the power to use the workings of comparative advantage, since it controls both imports and exports in a way which Western economies, committed to freer trade, do not, nevertheless its ability to do so is restricted by many practical limitations.

Another and equally fascinating subject, which I have to resist the temptation to discuss, is the position in the new trading blocs such as the EEC. Is this national or international business? On the one hand national sovereignties persist but on the other the objective is free movement of goods, capital and labour. Obviously this is a hybrid situation and is likely to remain so for many years. I do not think the analysis in this book is likely to be outdated for some little time as regards these new free-trade areas.

I hope finally that one thing at least is clear from the discussion in this book: that international business, as I said at the beginning, is an exceptionally exciting and interesting activity. The challenges which it offers tax fully the skills and abilities of even the best managers, and it is perhaps in this activity that many if not most of the leading managers of tomorrow will win their spurs.

Index

Management Series